QM2

A PHOTOGRAPHIC JOURNEY

(Courtesy of Cunard Line)

QM2

A PHOTOGRAPHIC JOURNEY

CHRIS FRAME AND RACHELLE CROSS

WITH AN AFTERWORD BY COMMODORE RYND, MASTER OF QM2

WITH CONTRIBUTIONS FROM
COMMODORE R.W. WARWICK &
COMMODORE BERNARD WARNER

The History Press

For George, John, Lil and Val

First published 2009
This edition published 2014

The History Press
The Mill
Brimscombe Port
Stroud
Gloucestershire
GL5 2QG
www.thehistorypress.co.uk

British Library Cataloguing in Publication Data.
A catalogue record for this book is available from the British Library.

ISBN 978-0-7509-5624-6
Typesetting and origination by The History Press
Printed in India

CONTENTS

FOREWORD

BY COMMODORE R.W. WARWICK

In April 1998, after months of speculation, the Carnival Corporation acquired Cunard Line, and, within a few weeks of doing so, the new owners announced their proposal to build an ocean liner. This ship soon became known as the *Queen Mary 2*.

After years of meticulous research and planning, a contract was signed with Chantiers de l'Atlantique, Saint Nazaire, to build the biggest ocean liner the world has ever known. From then on construction progressed with thousands of tons of steel and machinery being delivered to the builders of the ship assigned the yard number G32. On 4 July 2002, exactly 162 years to the day of the maiden voyage of the paddle steamer *Britannia*, Samuel Cunard's first ship, I had the honour of giving the order to lay the first keel section of my new ship, the *Queen Mary 2*.

Several months later I set up residence in Saint Nazaire and watched the vessel grow at a very rapid pace. It was exciting to see the architects' and designers' visions of grandeur and elegance becoming a reality. On the Bridge and in the Engine Room the latest in maritime and communications technology was being installed to make this new ship the most advanced ocean liner of our time.

On 22 December 2003, eighteen months after the keel was laid, the ship was formally handed over to Cunard Line, and, with only the crew on board, we bid farewell to Saint Nazaire and set sail for Vigo, Spain. For the next few days the crew and I had the ship totally to ourselves to carry out an intensive series of trials and tests. We docked the ship several times and turned her around in her own length using the azimuth-podded propulsion system and bow thrusters. The mooring arrangements, watertight doors and gas turbines were tested. The gangways and tender platforms were rigged. Lifeboats and tenders were launched. The anchors were lowered and emergency drills were carried out.

Meanwhile, the Hotel Department were busy preparing cabins and testing all the culinary facilities. The Britannia Restaurant was 'tested' by 1,000 crew members as we sailed across the Bay of Biscay on Christmas Day, bound for our maiden arrival at Southampton.

These few days of dedicated service by an incredibly proud and enthusiastic crew laid the foundations to introduce the magnificent *Queen Mary 2* to the world, and to perpetuate the reign of Cunard Liners on the North Atlantic.

In the ensuing five years, *Queen Mary 2* has travelled the world, sailed over 800,000 nautical miles and carried many thousands of passengers. Among those passengers have been Chris Frame and Rachelle Cross. I first met Chris on the *Queen Elizabeth 2* in 1998 during the World Cruise. As a youngster of thirteen, he was very interested in the ship, and as a result visited me on board during our call to Australia. A manifestation of this interest resulted in his widely acclaimed first book, *QE2 – A Photographic Journey*. It is therefore very fitting that Rachelle and Chris have applied their talents to this new book; a tribute to *Queen Mary 2*, the largest passenger liner ever built, as indeed the ship herself is a tribute to Cunard Line and all that the company is famous for.

I commend Chris and Rachelle for their dedication in celebrating the first five years of the *QM2* by recording this occasion for maritime history in pictorial form. I wish readers and travellers bon voyage as they turn these pages and sail the oceans of the world.

Commodore R.W. Warwick
Somerset
May 2009

Far left: (Courtesy of Andy Fitzsimmons)

Left: (Courtesy of Sam Warwick)

Right: (Courtesy of Cunard Line)

ACKNOWLEDGEMENTS

We are extremely grateful to everyone who helped us create this book. Special thanks go to: **Commodore R.W. Warwick** for writing the Foreword and providing photographic assistance; **Commodore B. Warner** for allowing us access to the 'behind the scenes' areas of *QM2* and providing us with his perspective of commanding the ship; **Commodore Rynd** for writing the Afterword; **Captain N. Bates** for his insight into the operations of the *QM2*; all of the **officers and crew of *QM2*** who helped us with tours of the ship and behind the scenec access; **Christel Hansen** and **Emily Wealleans** for organising the magnificent tours, photographic and informational assistance and your company aboard; **Michael Gallagher** and **Caroline Matheson** of the Cunard Line for their support in our writing and maritime lecture endeavours, as well as **Dragana Prodanovic** – *QM2* Voyage Sales Specialist – for your company aboard; **Amy Rigg**, **Emily Locke**, **Chrissy McMorris**, **Glad Stockdale** and **Lauren Newby**, our amazing team at The History Press, for your ongoing support and assistance in our books; **John Langley**, chairman of the Cunard Steamship Society, for his insight into the Boston Cup; **Bill Miller** for his ongoing support and kindness as well as everyone at *The QE2 Story Forum* for sharing their *QM2* passenger anecdotes and for their kind support; **Andy Fitzsimmons**, **Colin Hargreaves**, **Pam Massey**, **Kevin Moss**, **Sam Warwick**, **Stephen Hartley** and **Steve Jensen** for their photographic assistance, **George** for always being ready to go on a cruise, and our families for supporting us.

All photographs, unless otherwise acknowledged, were taken by Chris Frame or Rachelle Cross.

A ROYAL INTRODUCTION

To take a journey aboard the *Queen Mary 2* is to experience an age when travel was a leisurely pursuit. Despite being built decades after the Golden Age of the ocean liner, *QM2* offers passengers the precious gift of time, as she sails majestically across the world's oceans.

During a crossing or cruise, you'll mingle with your fellow passengers, creating new and lasting friendships. Dinner companions will share stories of their lives at home, their jobs, hobbies and interests. You'll meet new friends at tea, at bingo, in the Mayfair Shops or while taking a stroll on the promenade. As you get to know your new friends, your time aboard will take on a life of its own.

Soon you'll notice the shipboard community come alive. You'll say hello to people you don't know in the lift and trade thoughts about last night's production show, or this afternoon's planetarium movie. You'll make plans to meet your new friends for lunch in the Kings Court, or for afternoon tea in the Queens Room.

As the voyage progresses, passengers begin to forget their day-to-day lives back at home. News from far away lands is available, but often ignored as passengers become more and more involved in their newfound life at sea.

Within a few days you'll have a shipboard routine. Despite the size of the ship, you'll know your way around. You'll have your favourite 'parts of town'. Some passengers prefer the Commodore Club with its spectacular forward views. Others enjoy the comfort and elegance of the Chart Room. You'll be familiar with the crew and share conversations with them as the ship ploughs her way towards your final port of call. All too quickly, discussions will turn towards the destination, as your days aboard *QM2* draw to a close. Slowly, time catches up, and you'll find yourself trading address details, talking of onward flights or hotel arrangements, until, eventually, you're standing on the deck admiring *QM2*'s remarkable manoeuvrability as she makes berth.

Despite the tinge of sadness as you say goodbye to your adopted community, there will be an overwhelming feeling of happiness at the fact that you have been part of history, you've

(Photographs courtesy
of Andy Fitzsimmons)

sailed aboard the magnificent *QM2*, the last link to a time when a voyage by ship was the only way to travel.

This book offers you a chance to experience *QM2* whenever the mood strikes. Through these pages you can visit your favourite bars or lounges, walk the Promenade Deck, take in the planetarium and learn a bit about what makes *QM2* a true successor to the Cunard legacy.

A ROYAL PEDIGREE

There was a time, not so long ago, when ocean liners were the only way to travel. The ports around the world were bustling hives of activity; with liner after liner tied alongside taking on fuel, food and passengers. The passenger ship trade was a lucrative business and many companies fought to be the market leader on every ocean of the world. The likes of P&O, Orient Line, Blue Funnel and the Union Castle Line were all masters of their respective markets and won fame and fortune in the cities and countries which they served.

However, on one ocean the race for supremacy was not simply a matter of profits but also of national pride. The transatlantic was without question the most prestigious route that a shipping company could operate.

By far one of the most untamed beasts in the world, the North Atlantic had long allured entrepreneurs who could see the potential profits to be made by operating a regular scheduled service from the old world to the new. But it wasn't until 1839 that the technology, government and business plan aligned to make this service a reality.

Born in Halifax, Nova Scotia, Sir Samuel Cunard is the father of the transatlantic crossing. Answering a call from the British Government to provide a regular mail service, he won not only the Royal Mail contract but also the right to transport passengers on his ships. In 1840, when his first ship, *Britannia*, set sail on her maiden voyage the world became a smaller place and everything changed.

Within decades there was fierce competition on the Atlantic waters and Cunard faced opposition on many fronts. Be it the ill-fated Collins Line from the USA, or the magnificence of the German Norddeutsche Lloyd Line, the opulence of White Star or the speed and size of Hamburg-Amerika, Cunard fought on, maintaining a culture of safety first and speed second.

Despite putting safety first, Cunard's ships were by no means slow. In fact their 'ocean greyhounds' of the early 1900s, *Lusitania* and *Mauretania*, were easily the fastest liners in the world, a record *Mauretania* held for twenty-two years.

Cunard faced renewed competition with the introduction of the White Star Line's *Olympic*, while in Germany, construction of the *Imperator* would result in the largest and most majestic ship of her day.

Not to be outdone, Cunard commissioned the construction of their largest ship yet. Although slightly slower than her fleet mates, the *Aquitania* would be renowned as the most beautiful ship in the world, a reputation that earned her the nickname 'Ship Beautiful'.

Lusitania, *Mauretania*, *Aquitania*, *Olympic* and *Imperator* duelled with one-another in a tense but friendly rivalry until the onset of the First World War. After the war the lines set about re-establishing their routes and regaining their dominance. National pride was at stake and the developing powers in Europe used ocean liners to showcase their country's strength.

Born out of the growing tension between Europe and Great Britain were some of the finest liners ever to set sail. Germany started the race with the construction of the *Bremen* and *Europa*. Fast, sleek, powerful and, beyond all else, modern, the duo quickly won the Blue Riband as the fastest ships on the Atlantic.

In response, the Italians launched their flagship the *Rex*. She performed admirably and for a brief time traded the speed record with her German rivals. However, their supremacy would be short lived, as in France the world 's largest liner was under construction in Saint Nazaire. To be named the *Normandie*, she was a spectacular liner in every aspect. The world's largest, fastest and most opulent passenger ship, *Normandie* would win over the hearts and minds of passengers on both sides of the North Atlantic.

(Courtesy of Andy Fitzsimmons)

By the early 1930s Britain found herself in an embarrassing position. The world's strongest maritime power had no contender for the Blue Riband, having been surpassed by all of her rivals. However, Britain had hope in an unfinished hull, rusting on a slipway at the John Brown Shipyard in Scotland.

A casualty of the Great Depression, the rusting hull was destined to become one of the greatest Cunarders of all time. An agreement between Cunard and their once rival White Star Line allowed for an injection of desperately needed cash from the British Admiralty. By 1934 work had recommenced and the great liner, known simply as No.534, began to near completion.

To the delight of the British people, No.534 was named *Queen Mary* and took her place on the Atlantic as the unquestioned Queen of the Sea. She was fast, very fast, and won the Blue Riband back for Britain and Cunard.

(Courtesy of Colin Hargreaves)

Queen Mary was later joined by a larger sister the *Queen Elizabeth*, and the two Queens allowed Cunard to realise their long held ambition of a two-ship weekly transatlantic service. Throughout the 1940s and 1950s Cunard experienced its Golden Age. Things couldn't be better, or so it seemed.

Across the Atlantic in the United States of America, Boeing was putting the finishing touches on their 707 aircraft, which would revolutionise international travel. Within a decade the Cunard Queens, along with many of their rivals, would find themselves out of date and unwanted, destined for retirement, mothballs or the scrapyard.

Cunard, however, was unwilling to admit defeat. Despite dabbling in air travel in a joint venture with BOAC (now British Airways), Cunard opted to rely on a new design of passenger ship. Built as a dual-purpose liner, the company commissioned the magnificent *Queen Elizabeth 2*, which entered service in 1969.

Considered, for much of her life, as the last of the great transatlantic liners, *QE2* became a floating celebrity, earning instant notoriety at every port she visited. A classic tribute to the past, people all over the world were taken aback by her elegant, majestic appearance, while enjoying a lifestyle aboard seldom found elsewhere in the age of the jet.

By the mid-1990s it appeared as if the age of the transatlantic crossing was in its dying days. Cunard was in financial strain, battling an ageing fleet and lack of investment from their owners. However, in 1998 the future of Samuel Cunard's legacy was secured when Carnival Corporation purchased Cunard Line for an impressive US$800m.

Not only was the company's future safe, but when Cunard then announced Project Queen Mary – the construction of the largest ocean liner of all time, it seemed that the transatlantic service was safe for the foreseeable future.

Project Queen Mary developed to become *Queen Mary 2*, a grand liner of epic proportions. Her size is mind-boggling, at over five times longer than the first Cunard ship, *Britannia*. Built at the same shipyard as the famed *Normandie*, *QM2* incorporated the ultimate in modern technology, while still achieving a pleasing balance between modern creature comforts, and old world charm.

With the introduction of *QM2* into service in January 2004 (having been christened by HM Queen Elizabeth II), Cunard could boast once again the most modern and luxurious ship in the world.

WELCOME ABOARD

Your first experience of *QM2*'s grandeur begins the moment you enter the appropriately named Grand Lobby. The atrium spans five decks and is a wonder of gold hues, glass and glossy wood. Twin curved staircases allow access between Decks 2 and 3, while on the wall above there is a three-storey, polished aluminium bas-relief of the *QM2* on a rising sun. The artwork was created by Scottish artist John McKenna.

You can take in the atrium from the Grand Lobby itself, or see it from different angles by using the glass walled lifts that run from Deck 2 to Deck 7. *QM2* boasts atrium accommodation on Decks 4, 5 and 6, with windows that face inwards offering a unique perspective for those passengers with this grade of cabin. With its awe inspiring size and elegant décor, the Grand Lobby provides the perfect backdrop for formal photographs. It is a popular place for friends to meet before adjourning to one of the nearby bars and lounges.

F rom the sweeping elegance of the grand duplex suites to the cosy comfort of an interior cabin, there is accommodation aboard *QM2* to suit most budgets. Cabins are grouped into categories depending on such factors as whether they have windows or balconies, the size of the cabins and the availability of other amenities such as a bath tub.

Each category has a price which reflects these differences. All cabin grades provide twenty-four-hour room service, a nightly turndown service, daily replenished toiletries and everyone's favourite, a chocolate on your pillow before bed.

During the course of your voyage you'll get to know your cabin steward (or butler in Queens Grill accommodation) who will provide friendly, efficient service to help make your stay memorable.

DID YOU KNOW?

78 per cent of *QM2*'s cabins have a balcony.

Opposite page, middle right: (Courtesy of Stephen Hartley)

Oscar Mendoza, *QM2* butler.

QUEENS GRILL ACCOMMODATION

The highest level of comfort aboard *QM2* is found in the Queens Grill suites, penthouses and duplex apartments. In addition to having the most luxurious accommodation on board, guests travelling in this grade enjoy the services of a butler and complimentary mini bar as well as access to the Queens Grill Lounge and Queens Grill Sun Deck.

The Grand Duplexes, aptly named Balmoral and Sandringham (after royal residences) are the most magnificent suites aboard. These apartment-style rooms span two decks and offer spacious living areas, separate bedroom, two extravagant walk-in robes, marble bathrooms and a private deck as well as a butler's pantry!

Top left: (Courtesy of Stephen Hartley)

PRINCESS GRILL ACCOMMODATION

(Courtesy of Steve Jensen)

Those passengers seeking a more lavish cruise experience can select Princess Grill Accommodation. These suites are more spacious than Britannia Accommodation, with the added pleasure of a bath as well as shower.

Princess Grill occupants will enjoy access to the exclusive Queens Grill Lounge on Deck 7, as well as the Concierge Lounge on Deck 12.

Asked of a Cabin Steward:

How do you get to work in the morning?

BRITANNIA & BRITANNIA CLUB ACCOMMODATION

DID YOU KNOW?

There are 46 Britannia Club cabins aboard *QM2*.

Asked of a Deck 8 Cabin Steward:

Can you lower the lifeboat?
It's blocking our view!

The majority of *QM2*'s passengers sail in Britannia accommodation which ranges in style and spaciousness, from comfortable interior cabins to deluxe balcony staterooms. The cabins are finished in a relaxing neutral colour scheme with queen beds, which can be easily converted into two large singles.

For those seeking an extra level of comfort, the Britannia Club category offers additional luxuries including daily fresh fruit delivery and a shoe-shine service. Britannia Club cabins are located on Deck 12 with a full size balcony, and guests in these rooms dine in the more intimate Britannia Club Restaurant.

RESTAURANTS

You'll never go hungry on *QM2*! In addition to the twenty-four-hour room service menu provided in your cabin, you can choose to eat in your allocated restaurant, the buffet style Kings Court Restaurant or the more private Todd English Restaurant.

Light meals, lunch and cakes are also available at other locations around the ship. In fact there are so many dining choices aboard *QM2*, chances are you won't get an opportunity to try them all!

RESTAURANT PROFILE

Restaurant	Location	Rating
Queens Grill	Deck 7 (Starboard)	5 Star
Princess Grill	Deck 7 (Port)	5 Star
Britannia Club	Deck 2	4 Star
Britannia Restaurant	Deck 2 and 3	4 Star
Kings Court	Deck 7	Alfresco
Todd English Restaurant	Deck 8	5 Star
Boardwalk Café	Deck 12	Alfresco

Opposite, right: (Courtesy of Steve Jensen)

QUEENS GRILL

Rated as one of the finest dining experiences at sea the Queens Grill Restaurant is located starboard, aft on Deck 7. This restaurant offers an extensive menu and stellar service which is often compared to the finest restaurants on land.

The Queens Grill is decorated in gold hues with an intimate atmosphere and offers single seating service, allowing guests to dine at their leisure.

DID YOU KNOW?

Guests dining in the Queens Grill are welcome to order dishes not shown on the menu.

PRINCESS GRILL

Catering to those travelling in the Princess Grill suites, this restaurant is decorated with silver finishes and has a view onto the port Promenade Deck. Offering elegant fine dining in a single seating atmosphere, the Princess Grill has a private feel due largely to curtained partitions, giving the illusion that the room is smaller than it actually is.

Guests eating in the Princess Grill will enjoy an extensive menu served by highly trained wait staff, offering the utmost in silver service. Sommeliers are on hand to offer advice on wine selection to complement the meal.

BRITANNIA & BRITANNIA CLUB RESTAURANTS

One of the most visually striking rooms aboard *QM2*, the Britannia Restaurant spans three decks. It offers four levels of seating accessed by curved staircases and is complemented by an ornate glass ceiling. A giant tapestry by Barbara Broekman dominates the aft wall and depicts a *Queen Mary/Queen Mary 2* hybrid set amid skyscrapers and the Brooklyn Bridge in New York.

The Britannia Restaurant serves breakfast and lunch in an open seating arrangement and dinner in two sittings, with allocated tables of varying sizes.

The restaurant is decorated in a style that brings to mind the romantic ideal of ocean liner travel, which is emphasised by the inclusion of the Captain's Table on the Deck 2 level of this restaurant.

Those diners from Britannia Club Accommodation will find a table reserved for them in a separate intimate section of the Britannia Restaurant. This area, known as the Britannia Club Restaurant, is found on the lower level at the rear port side and offers single seating dining.

DID YOU KNOW?

The Britannia Restaurant can cater for up to 1,200 people in a single sitting.

KINGS COURT

A buffet-style eatery at breakfast and lunch times, the Kings Court Restaurant is divided into four distinct sections, which, although connected, are also uniquely decorated. These areas are the Asian-inspired Lotus, Italian offering La Piazza, British-style Carvery and the Chef's Galley where you can watch the chefs prepare gastronomic delights right before your eyes.

Heard on Deck 7:

What time is the midnight buffet?

On any night up to three of these options will serve a la carte and require a booking to be made. During buffet service, this restaurant can be hard to navigate, with various seating alcoves spread throughout the restaurant. Despite the initial confusion, passengers always manage to find a satisfying meal.

TODD ENGLISH RESTAURANT

Another popular alternative dining venue is the Todd English Restaurant. Decorated in a bold colour palette, Todd English is situated at the aft end of Deck 8 with an alfresco area on the teak wood decking by the Terrace Pool.

With a menu designed by its namesake (renowned chef Todd English) this restaurant offers Mediterranean cuisine not found in any of the other restaurants aboard. Eating at this restaurant is not included in the standard cruise fare and incurs a cover charge.

Due to its popularity, it is recommended that you make a telephone booking for the Todd English Restaurant.

BOARDWALK CAFÉ

If you're feeling peckish but don't fancy a sit-down meal then head to the Boardwalk Café. The highest restaurant aboard *QM2* (by altitude), the Boardwalk Café is a buffet-style eatery which serves salads, light grill dishes and desserts in a casual atmosphere.
Open when the weather is pleasant, seating is placed out on the deck so passengers can take in the panoramic views while enjoying a casual but delicious meal.

BARS AND LOUNGES

BAR AND LOUNGE PROFILE

Bars and Lounges	Location
Regatta Bar	Deck 13
The Pavilion Bar	Deck 12
Atlantic Room	Deck 11
Commodore Club	Deck 9
Boardroom	Deck 9
Churchill's	Deck 9
Concierge Lounge	Deck 9
Terrace Bar	Deck 8
Winter Garden	Deck 7
Queens Grill Lounge	Deck 7
Veuve Clicquot Champagne Bar	Deck 3
Sir Samuel's	Deck 3
Chart Room	Deck 3
Queens Room	Deck 3
G32	Deck 3
Empire Casino	Deck 2
Golden Lion	Deck 2

In between meal times and shore days most passengers find time to relax and enjoy the atmosphere of *QM2*'s many bars and lounges. It's not all peace and quiet though! You can try your hand at roulette in the Empire Casino, party hard in the G32 nightclub or dance the night away at a deck party. And if you can still find the space to squeeze in just a little more to eat (and why not, it's a holiday) then you can enjoy high tea in the Queens Room.

REGATTA BAR

The Regatta Bar is located just below the mast on Deck 13. Boasting spectacular views and the highest vantage point on the ship, the Regatta Bar is the perfect place to enjoy the sun whilst sipping your favourite drink. And if the heat gets too much, you can cool off in the splash pool just aft of the bar.

DID YOU KNOW?

The decking aboard *QM2* is teak wood.

THE PAVILION BAR

The Pavilion Bar on Deck 12 is a great place for a by-the-pool beverage. This bar serves a variety of drinks overlooking the Pavilion Pool which can be covered by a sliding glass roof in inclement weather.

There are two table tennis tables here, as well as plenty of deck chairs for passengers to relax on. The Fairways, *QM2*'s golf simulator, is accessed from the aft end of The Pavilion.

ATLANTIC ROOM

Nestled high atop the ship on Deck 11 you'll find the Atlantic Room. Its forward location allows this area to benefit from sweeping views overlooking the Observation Deck.

Due to its intimate nature, the Atlantic Room is used for a variety of purposes including small cocktail parties and bridge lessons as well as holding services for the Sabbath for Jewish passengers at sundown on Fridays.

COMMODORE CLUB

Located at the forward end of Deck 9, the Commodore Club has full length angled windows which follow the curve of the ship and allow guests to see the horizons ahead. The Commodore Club has a relaxed and elegant atmosphere and is a popular location to sip a cocktail in the evening, with Martinis being the speciality. Behind the bar there is a scale model of the *QM2* by Dutch model-maker Henk Brandwijk.

THE POPULAR PASSIONADA MARTINI

2 parts vodka,
3 parts passion fruit juice (strained pulp),
Shake with plenty of ice and serve in a sugar-rimmed Martini glass.

(Courtesy of Steve Jensen)

BOARDROOM

Just aft of the Commodore Club on the port side is the Boardroom. A small room, it can be used for meetings, but is more often in use as a quiet lounge.

The room has large windows and a mirrored wall, making it bright during the day, and an electric fireplace, giving it a very cosy atmosphere in the evenings.

CHURCHILL'S

Following the worldwide trend, *QM2*'s public rooms are largely non-smoking. One prominent exception is Churchill's. A small lounge with dark wood cabinets and heavy furniture, the Cigar Room is comfortable, with an appearance evocative of an exclusive members' only club in London.

CONCIERGE LOUNGE

Reminiscent of an exclusive airline club, the Concierge Lounge is open for passengers travelling in Queens or Princess Grill Accommodation. As one would expect, given its name, the Concierge Lounge is where Grill guests will find their personal concierge service which covers general shipboard information, shore excursion bookings and account queries.

Light refreshments and newspapers from around the world are in popular demand, while other passengers prefer the quiet and secluded atmosphere for checking their emails via the ships WiFi service.

TERRACE BAR & POOL

Located at the aft of Deck 8, directly behind the Todd English Restaurant, is the Terrace Bar. Overlooking the Terrace Pool and the endless blue of the ocean, the Terrace Bar is the location of 'sail away' parties when leaving ports. The pool is surrounded by a bandstand with a built-in sound system, allowing passengers to enjoy music in a party atmosphere thanks to the ship's own Caribbean band.

When sailing across the equator, it is traditional for a passenger ship to host King Neptune and his Court. The Terrace Pool is the preferred location for the age-old ceremony which sees those who have never crossed the equator (Pollywogs) transformed into those who have (Shellbacks).

CROSSING THE LINE

Although considered a fun event aboard passenger ships, the 'Crossing the Line' ceremony has a darker history. Nineteenth-century sailors were often subject to beatings whilst crossing the line. Others were tied to a rope and thrown overboard to be dragged through the ocean. By comparison, the worst thing you're likely to encounter aboard *QM2* is the requirement to 'kiss the fish'.

WINTER GARDEN

A tranquil and welcoming retreat, the Winter Garden is the location for the *QM2*'s art auctions, which is appropriate as the room is a work of art in itself. The ceiling and several of the walls have been painted in garden-themed murals. The garden atmosphere is accentuated by potted plants, wicker furniture and flower printed upholstery, while the main focal point of the Winter Garden is a water feature on the aft bulkhead. At night, the Winter Garden is transformed into a magical paradise by the use of blue lighting, giving it an elegant evening ambience.

DID YOU KNOW?

The Winter Garden has a self-playing piano.

QUEENS GRILL LOUNGE

Elegant and understated could be two of the watchwords of *QM2*'s Queens Grill Lounge. Tastefully decorated in neutral shades, the room is set aside for the exclusive use of Princess and Queens Grill passengers.

The Queens Grill Lounge has a full bar and serves pre- and post-dinner drinks, as well as providing high tea in the afternoons. The Queens Grill Lounge is located just forward of the Queens Grill on Deck 7.

VEUVE CLICQUOT CHAMPAGNE BAR

For a glamorous and sophisticated experience try the Veuve Clicqout Champagne Bar on Deck 3. Black and white images of Hollywood legends adorn two walls, with most of the room open to the Grand Lobby.

Passengers who enjoy people watching will find this bar a comfortable place to sit and watch the other guests go by, while others will savour the view from large windows facing out to the ocean.

Those with an appreciation for fine wine can enjoy the various Veuve Clicquot champagnes on offer, or, if that doesn't appeal, can access the drinks menu from the neighbouring Chart Room.

Below right: (Courtesy of Steve Jensen)

SIR SAMUEL'S WINE BAR

The image of Sir Samuel Cunard, founder of the Cunard Line, watches over guests in this bar. Aft of the Mayfair Shops on the port side of Deck 3, Sir Samuel's is a dual-purpose room.

Specialty coffee and light meals are served during the day, while at night the room becomes the *QM2*'s wine bar and is a great place to experience a selection of *QM2*'s cellar. Decorated in warm tones, Sir Samuel's is a favourite with many guests.

CHART ROOM

N amed after the room on *QE2*, the Chart Room on *QM2* is one of the most popular bars aboard and the fastest to fill up in the evenings. Light wood panelling and aqua glass charts offset against traditional Latin maps give the Chart Room a distinctive flavour.

A peaceful retreat, the Chart Room has large windows, providing magnificent views by day. During the evenings passengers will enjoy the comfortable chairs while partaking in pre-dinner drinks to the sound of live musical performances.

DID YOU KNOW?

QM2 is the flagship of the Cunard Line.

QUEENS ROOM

A ft of the Britannia Restaurant on Deck 3 is the Queens Room. The epitome of British indulgence is the white-gloved high tea served here every afternoon. Though first time guests sometimes have difficulty finding their way here, it is never more than a few days after embarkation before the room is filled to capacity.

This relaxed and elegant lounge is not just popular during the daylight hours. In the evening guests can dance to the live band on the largest dance floor at sea. On special occasions the room is transformed and plays host to cocktail parties and themed balls.

G32

G32 is the *QM2*'s nightclub and is located at the aft of the ship. You enter the nightclub through the Queens Room on Deck 3 and from there can make your way up to Deck 3L via two staircases. From this vantage point it is possible to look back into the Queens Room from internal portholes. G32 has atmospheric lighting and a smoke machine, making it a great place to dance the night away. Music is supplied by a DJ and a live dance band.

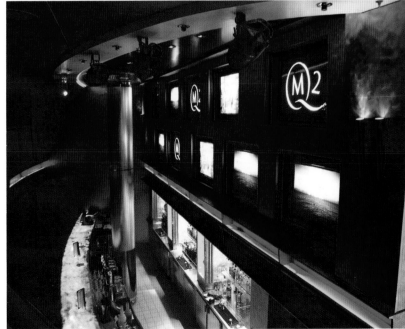

EMPIRE CASINO

I f Lady Luck is on your side there is ample opportunity to win money on the *QM2*. Located amidships on Deck 2, the Empire Casino offers a wide selection of gaming tables and slot machines. Vegas-style neon lights are juxtaposed against murals on the forward wall of a period gambling scene, featuring immaculately dressed gentlemen and elegant female partners.

The Casino is open from 10 a.m. on sea days (the tables open at 11) with world regulations keeping it closed whilst the ship is in port. Drinks are available at the Casino Bar and guests can enjoy participating in regular themed events including the popular 007 night.

GOLDEN LION PUB

Traditional British fare is what's on offer for lunch at the Golden Lion Pub. Guests can tuck into fish and chips with mushy peas, a ploughman's lunch, a cottage pie or a warming curry.

The Golden Lion Pub also serves beer and ale on tap and offers live music and karaoke. With a relaxed and friendly atmosphere and a décor tending heavily towards wood finishes, reds and dark greens, the Golden Lion is a favourite with many passengers.

PUBLIC AREAS

The *QM2* boasts an outstanding array of facilities for relaxation, entertainment and enrichment. As well as having the only planetarium at sea, the *QM2* also has a world-class spa, gymnasium and beauty centre. If you fancy unwinding with a book in a quiet spot you'll find what you're looking for in the Library and if you want something to remind you of your trip, souvenirs can be purchased right next door in the Bookshop. Duty free items can be purchased in the Mayfair Shops and if by the end of the day you find yourself exhausted and in need of a pick me up then you need do no more than slide into a seat at the Royal Court Theatre, order a cocktail and watch a live show that will electrify you.

PARTICULAR AREAS OF INTEREST:

Name	Location
The Library	Deck 8
QM2 Bookshop	Deck 8
Canyon Ranch Spaclub	Deck 8 & Deck 7
Canyon Ranch Gym	Deck 7
The Zone	Deck 6
The Mayfair Shops	Deck 3
Illuminations	Deck 3
Royal Court Theatre	Deck 3 & Deck 2
Gallery and Images	Deck 3L
The Pursers Office	Deck 2
ConneXions	Deck 2
Tender Lounges	Deck 1
Laundrettes	Most passenger decks
Maritime Quest	Everywhere

THE LIBRARY

Book lovers rejoice! *QM2* has one of the largest libraries at sea, with over 8,000 titles lining the shelves. The Library is open during the day for passengers to browse and check books out. There are also magazines and newspapers to while away a pleasant afternoon. If you can tear your eyes away from perusing the shelves, you will discover that the Library has excellent forward facing views.

By night the glass doors are pulled closed and locked over the books so that the Library can remain in use as a quiet lounge and internet access point.

With its peaceful atmosphere and plethora of reading materials it is little wonder that many passengers remember the Library with great fondness.

QM2 BOOKSHOP

If there aren't enough books in the Library to tempt you, or you just want a souvenir to show your friends at home, the *QM2* Bookshop, just aft of the Library, should be your next port of call.

Stocked with a wide range of maritime books as well as bookmarks, card decks, pens and posters, the *QM2* Bookshop most likely has exactly what you're looking for. The *QM2* Bookshop also stocks a small range of novels and other genre books, if you are looking for something to fill the hours on the journey home.

CANYON RANCH SPACLUB

The *QM2* boasts the only Canyon Ranch Spaclub at sea. Spanning two decks at the forward end of the ship, the Canyon Ranch Spaclub offers the ultimate in indulgence. The spa complex allows passengers to relax in a tranquil setting and includes a thalasotherapy pool, private whirlpool and beauty centre. Spa patrons can partake of massages, body wrap treatments and health checks.

The beauty centre, on Deck 8, is accessed via a staircase set amid a tropical theme. Hairdressing, manicures, pedicures and makeup services are on offer here. With a number of formal nights on each *QM2* voyage, the beauty centre staff are kept busy with a steady stream of patrons.

CANYON RANCH GYM

For the health conscious passengers and those who worry that their formal wear might not fit at the end of the cruise, the *QM2* has a fully equipped gym and weights room for guests to enjoy. Located at the forward end of Deck 7, it is by no means the most popular room on board, but it nonetheless remains in almost constant use throughout the day.

Personal trainers are on hand to design individual exercise programs. For those who are willing to make the effort it is possible to be in better shape at the end of your holiday than you were at the beginning.

THE ZONE

Parents, relax! *QM2* is fully catered to look after your kids and provide them with an exciting and enjoyable cruise experience. The ship offers a range of activities for youngsters at The Zone, which is located on Deck 6, aft.

The Play Zone acts as both a crèche and child-care centre. Staffed by a team of British nannies, The Play Zone offers a safe and secure retreat for little ones, while keeping them entertained in a fun nursery environment.

For older kids The Zone offers a wide variety of toys and games as well as computer terminals packed full of fun (and educational) activities. The Zone is within easy reach of Minnows, the specialty children's outdoor activity area.

With sweeping views over the stern of *QM2*, Minnows has a pool, fountain and water-pistol platform as well as other kid's games such as hop-scotch and a cubby house located on the deck nearby.

MAYFAIR SHOPS

Amidships on Deck 3, bordering the Grand Lobby, are the Mayfair Shops. This is the place to shop for duty free jewellery, perfume, designer clothing and alcohol. Some of the big name brands among *QM2*'s shops include Escada, Swarovski, Hermès and H. Stern.

With a glass frontage, light wood and gold finishes, you don't have to be travelling Queens Grill class to feel like a star here. The friendly staff and varied products on offer make shopping here an enjoyable and memorable experience.

ILLUMINATIONS

Almost all passengers sailing aboard *QM2* will visit Illuminations. This magnificent room not only holds the distinction of being the first planetarium at sea, but it also hosts a variety of events as a multi-purpose venue. In keeping with its planetary theme, the entrance of Illuminations is guarded by statues of Jupiter, Mercury, Andromeda and Cassandra. At the entrance, passengers can check out the daily schedule displayed on two large LCD screens.

On entering Illuminations, the room appears to be a large lecture theatre, as indeed it is. During days at sea, guest lecturers give talks on topics ranging from royalty to science to film stars and history. For planetarium shows a giant domed screen is lowered over the central seats and the shows are projected onto this dome. Guests avoid neck ache by reclining the (red) seats to offer a superb retrospective of the universe.

If it's less cerebral viewing you're craving, you can always catch new release and classic movies which are also shown here on a traditional cinema screen, which is lowered from the ceiling behind the main stage.

DID YOU KNOW?

QM2 completed her 200th transatlantic crossing in July 2013

ROYAL COURT THEATRE

A venue that always draws a crowd is the Royal Court Theatre. The *QM2*'s show lounge hosts production shows, musicians, dancers, comedians and other performers on a mechanised stage.

The Royal Court Theatre has seating over two levels, Deck 2 and Deck 3, offering passengers magnificent views of the performances. To accommodate the maximum number of guests, the Royal Court Theatre hosts two productions each night – one aimed at passengers who dine early, and the other for passengers who dine late.

While the entertainers who perform in this theatre are often only aboard for short segments, the quality of their performances ensures that they are remembered long after they have departed the ship.

PURSERS OFFICE

Starboard, on the lowest level of the Grand Lobby, is the Pursers Office. Responsible for passenger administration, all guests have contact with this office at some point during their cruise. The Pursers Office performs such varied tasks as compiling passenger accounts, replacing lost cruise cards, storing passports and ensuring all guests are aboard before the ship departs.

Staff at the Pursers Office are there to ensure that the cruise runs smoothly and work hard behind the scenes. *QM2*'s Pursers Office has a curved granite desk complemented by light wood panelling.

DID YOU KNOW?

Although there are several cruise ships larger than *QM2*, she is the longest, largest and most expensive ocean liner ever built.

GALLERY AND IMAGES

Running through the Britannia Restaurant on the cleverly hidden Deck 3L, you'll find *QM2*'s art gallery. The Gallery has wood-panelled walls and blue carpets, and has an overall feel of richness and luxury. Art works are displayed in the Gallery during the cruise and passengers can request to see favourite pieces at the auctions, held in the Winter Garden. Prior to the auction, the pieces are taken from the Gallery and returned upon completion.

On the port side of Deck 3L is Images, *QM2*'s Photo Gallery. All photos taken by the ship's photographers are displayed here. A twin room to the Gallery on the starboard side, Images is often extremely busy, with guests eager to see how their shots turned out. The photos displayed in Images are available for purchase along with stock photos of the *QM2*.

CONNEXIONS

I f you want to stay in touch with those on land and you aren't able to take advantage of the in-room wireless connection then you will find yourself at Cunard ConneXions.

Located just aft of the lower level of Illuminations, ConneXions offers computers with internet service (for a fee) in addition to being a learning centre.

ConneXions is made up of a number of smaller rooms, some that can be combined to form a larger room. The rooms are used for a variety of purposes including computer courses, bridge lessons, passport checks, language classes and as meeting areas for those travelling in groups.

ConneXions even has a recording studio, where the daily 'Good Morning QM2' programme is recorded.

Overheard in ConneXions:

Why doesn't the ship have cable?

TENDER LOUNGES

Due to her immense size, *QM2* often has to anchor when cruising to smaller ports. This results in passengers being taken ashore using one of *QM2*'s large catamaran tenders which are stored atop the Promenade Deck while at sea. Tender rides offer passengers spectacular views of the ship at anchor, but traditionally can cause long queues and delays while waiting for an available boat.

In order to reduce this inconvenience, *QM2* was built with four tender lounges located on Deck 1, which are named Kensington, Chelsea, Knightsbridge and Belgravia. These lounges offer a comfortable area for guests to wait for their tender ride. Each lounge is adorned with Cunard marketing posters from a bygone era while offering the comforts of cold drinks and bathrooms to ensure the wait is as pleasant as possible.

Large shell doors open outwards and act as a pontoon for easy boarding of the tender boats which simply pull alongside to embark and disembark passengers.

DID YOU KNOW?

QM2 has eight large catamaran tender boats, which can also act as lifeboats.

LAUNDERETTES

espite the fact that *QM2* offers a professional laundry service, some of the most frequented rooms aboard are the self-service Launderettes. There are several aboard the ship, spread across a variety of passenger decks. Each offers a number of washers and dryers as well as ironing boards for guests to use.

Regardless of the best of intentions, at peak times there is never quite enough space for all the passengers aboard, which results in some tense moments. It is not unknown for people to take matters into their own hands by barricading themselves in the Launderette and only allowing passengers from 'their' deck in.

From one passenger to another with great suspicion:

What deck are you from?!

MARITIME QUEST

Ship buffs won't be short of historical anecdotes aboard *QM2* with the Maritime Quest offering an abundance of information from Cunard's long history. Taking the form of a self-guided tour, the Maritime Quest offers historical snippets, amusing stories and famous faces through various presentations scattered about the corridors aboard.

At the forward end of Deck 2 the Maritime Quest reaches its climax with a number of touch screens offering an interactive experience, with facts, games and quizzes to test your knowledge.

DID YOU KNOW?

QM2's namesake, *Queen Mary*, holds the record for the most people carried in a single crossing, 16,082 during the Second World War.

Advice from a bygone era:

Seasickness Remedy – Eat nothing for twenty-four hours,
then drink Champagne. (Advice from a Cunard captain to
passengers, as depicted in the *Maritime Quest*.)

GETTING AROUND

On a ship the size of *QM2*, getting from point A to point B can sometimes require consultation with the deck plans. To make life as easy as possible, *QM2* was designed with four major stairways, providing access to the passenger decks. While taking the stairs is a great way to keep in shape, there are lifts provided at each of these stairways, making the trip a little less tiring.

Each of the stairways is colour coded allowing for simple identification of your location. The stairways provide access to the kilometres of corridors which connect the various public rooms, restaurants, bars, lounges and passenger accommodation.

The ship's corridors, lifts and stairways are decorated with artworks which make up a large percentage of *QM2*'s £3 million art collection.

HIDDEN IMAGE

The bas relief in the Deck 3 corridor (between the Grand Lobby and the Britannia Restaurant) which depicts North America has an image of Homer Simpson hidden in it!

ON DECK

As with most ships built in recent years, *QM2* provides plenty of scope for sun worshippers to get their fix. Seven of *QM2*'s decks provide open air spaces, four of which also have pools.

The decks are the perfect spot to take in the view, play shuffleboard and meet others. The Promenade Deck, located on Deck 7, is a popular location for a spot of exercise – three times around and you've walked a mile!

When entering and leaving ports the decks are the perfect place to snap some photos, wave at onlookers and appreciate the remarkable manoeuvrability of this giant liner.

Heard On Deck:

How long until it stops raining?

PARTICULAR AREAS OF INTEREST:

Location	Deck	Facilities (at or nearby)
The Lookout	Deck 13	Forward facing views
Sports Centre	Deck 13	Golf, basketball and tennis
Regatta Pool	Deck 13	The Regatta Bar, Sports Centre
The Pavilion Pool	Deck 12	The Pavilion Bar, table tennis, Fairways
Observation Decks	Deck 11 and Deck 7	Fantastic views
Terrace Pool	Deck 8	The Terrace Bar, Todd English, live band area
Promenade Deck	Deck 7	Ample deck chairs
Minnows	Deck 6	The Zone

THE LOOKOUT

Passengers wishing to get a 'Captain's Eye View' will enjoy The Lookout. Situated at the forward end of Deck 13, just above the Bridge, The Lookout is a sheltered observation platform with forward facing views.

The Lookout is popular with passengers for winter arrivals and departures due to its sheltered nature and offers an excellent location to experience the sound from *QM2*'s mast-mounted horn.

SPORTS CENTRE

The *QM2* offers a variety of sport activities, allowing passengers a greater chance of staying active during their voyage. The Sports Centre is located on Deck 13 and houses a range of these activities including the golf driving-range, paddle tennis and basketball courts.

Further aft, traditional shipboard games such as deck quoits can be found, while on Deck 12, next to the funnel, passengers can enjoy shuffleboard on one of four courts. Adjacent to the shuffleboard courts is the Pavilion Pool which is housed under a Magrodome (a glass sliding roof which can be closed in bad weather). Nearby, golfers will find the Fairways – a computerised golf simulator which allows you to perfect your swing on a number of world-class courses.

OBSERVATION DECKS

S ailing at sea aboard an ocean liner can offer a unique perspective of the world. Passengers undertaking traditional line voyages will marvel at the magnificence of the ocean while *QM2* ploughs through her natural element at speeds approaching 30 knots.

To accommodate the passengers' desire to take in this unique panorama, *QM2* has several well-placed Observation Decks. High atop the ship, located under the Bridge, one of these Observation Decks can be found. Enveloping the exterior wall of the Atlantic Room, this deck offers sweeping views over the ship's bow. This area extends over the side of the ship, offering spectacular views aft, making it an extremely popular location for viewing arrivals into ports of call.

DID YOU KNOW?

The first Cunard Queen was RMS *Queen Mary* of 1936.

Another area that attracts a crowd during arrivals and departures is the Deck 7 Observation Deck. Here you'll find interesting works of art, which are actually spare propeller blades mounted on the deck. The spares are carried aboard as it is far more economical to have them already with *QM2* should they be required, than having to fly replacements out to the ship.

This deck has forward views and also allows passengers the unique perspective of looking up at the superstructure of *QM2*.

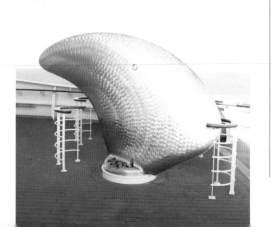

THE PROFILE

The first thing most people notice about *QM2* is her sheer size. At 1,132ft long, and with a gross tonnage of over 151,400 tons, she is the longest, tallest, widest and above all largest ocean liner ever built. Her design is nonetheless sleek and streamlined, with a long bow and bridge set high on the superstructure. These features, together with others not immediately visible (for example, the thickened hull and long bulbous bow) increase her efficiency on the world's oceans.

She is dressed in the traditional Cunard colours, with a matte-black hull, white superstructure and iconic red and black funnel. This distinctive colouring is not only practical (black paint on the hull doesn't show rust or chip marks easily, as well as absorbing heat on the chilly North Atlantic) it also brings to mind images of a bygone era, when ocean liners were the only way to travel.

DID YOU KNOW?

An ocean liner is different from a cruise ship as it undertakes regular scheduled line voyages between two ports.

THE FUNNEL

Instantly recognisable as Cunard, the funnel aboard *QM2* owes its shape to a design created three decades earlier with the construction of *QE2*. The design includes a central stack (the black part), the cowling (the red part) and an oversized 'scoop' at the forward base of the funnel.

The scoop is designed to push air up the outside of the funnel. As the ship moves through the water air is caught by the scoop and directed upwards. As the air passes the top of the stack it collects the soot and diesel exhaust fumes and carries them with it, up and away from the aft decks of the ship. This results in a more comfortable environment for sun bathers.

Although the original design was taken from the *QE2*, the funnel aboard *QM2* is by no means an exact replica. As *QM2* is considerably taller than her predecessor the funnel had to be shortened to allow the ship to pass under the Verrazano-Narrows Bridge in New York. As a result, *QM2*'s funnel, despite being 21m tall (from Deck 12 to the top), has a somewhat squat appearance.

> **DID YOU KNOW?**
>
> *QM2* sailed on her hundredth transatlantic crossing in September 2008.

THE WHISTLES

There are four whistles aboard *QM2*, one located on her bow, one on the mast and two set high atop the funnel. The whistles produce a deep bass 'A' note, giving *QM2* a distinctive voice which is audible for up to 16km (10 miles).

The starboard whistle on *QM2*'s funnel is an original from the *Queen Mary*, which was taken on permanent loan from the former Cunard Liner, now in retirement at Longbeach, California.

The port whistle is a replica created by Kockums Ab of Sweden – the manufacturers of the original whistles for *Queen Mary*.

DID YOU KNOW?

The *Queen Mary*'s whistle was transported from the USA to Europe aboard the *QE2*.

THE MAST

Situated atop the Bridge on Deck 13 you'll find the mast. Towering an impressive 62m from sea level, the mast aboard *QM2* takes its modern and stylised shape from her elder sister, *QE2*. This tradition in design is also continued aboard *Queen Victoria* and *Queen Elizabeth*.

Aside from its aesthetic importance, the mast serves a practical role. It carries an array of navigational technology required for manoeuvring the vessel, including the Global Positioning System (GPS), radar and radio transmitters.

Sailing tradition is maintained to the highest standard aboard Cunard ships, and the mast plays a significant role in flying the Cunard house flags, British Ensign (as *QM2* is registered in a British port), maritime signal flags and the flag of the port being visited.

QM2's mast, like her funnel, was originally intended to be taller, making it a more exact facsimile of *QE2*'s mast. During design, considerations such as the height of the ship and the need to pass under the Verrazano-Narrows Bridge in New York resulted in the mast being shortened, allowing *QM2* to complete the transatlantic service.

DID YOU KNOW?

Due to her length, *QM2* is no longer allowed to dock at the traditional Cunard piers in New York; instead she must dock in Brooklyn.

TRADITIONAL LINES

During the cruising resurgence in the late 1990s, passenger demands for greater creature comforts, more space and the option of a balcony resulted in new cruise ships being built with a far more angular appearance. While ocean liners of old were created with classic lines such as long bows and terraced sterns, the coast-hugging high density cruise ship took a form of function. The squarer shape of the cruise ships is more practical, as more cabins fit into a square than a circle.

QM2, having evolved from the ocean liner, was created not only to be as functional as possible, but also to survive the hostilities of a transatlantic crossing. As such, she adopted many features common with her ocean liner predecessors.

QM2 has a long bow, with her Bridge gracefully set back, high atop her superstructure. Her hull shape echoes the majestic curves of iconic liners such as the *Normandie* and

the *France*. Further aft, Cunard opted to give *QM2* magnificent terraced stern decks, with glass windscreens reminiscent of those that served so well aboard her predecessors.

While *QE2* had only a handful of balcony cabins, *QM2* has hundreds, and these are masterfully incorporated into the overall design, allowing the ship to maintain a graceful appearance while still offering world-class accommodation. From Deck 8 to Deck 12 the balconies are constructed in a traditional manner, offering panoramic views of the passing ocean.

Lower down, balcony cabins have been uniquely constructed with the creation of 'hull holes' whereby the balcony is totally sheltered within the hull. A large opening provides access to fresh air, while floor to ceiling glass doors shelter the cabin from the elements.

Topped by the traditional Cunard funnel and majestically-stylised mast, the overall effect is a modern vessel with an elegant silhouette recognised the world over.

DID YOU KNOW?

QM2's Bridge Wings were extended during her 2006 refurbishment to allow for greater visibility.

THE BREAKWATER

One of the most distinguishing features of *QM2* is her Breakwater. Set at the forward end of Deck 7, the Breakwater takes its shape from a design created in the 1920s for the French liner *Normandie*.

QM2 was constructed at the same shipyard as the *Normandie* and, although being worlds apart from the former French Line flagship, the design of the Breakwater serves the same purpose. Its primary function is to deflect water away from the superstructure, thus protecting the ship from the intensity of the North Atlantic Ocean.

Aside from its practical aspect, the Breakwater complements the appearance of *QM2*, offering a strong connection between the modern design of this ship and the classic liners of days gone by.

Behind the scenes there is an army of over 1,250 people working tirelessly to ensure that your voyage aboard *QM2* is enjoyable, exceptional and beyond all, memorable. While staff at a hotel on land can return home after a long day's work, the crew aboard *QM2* need to eat, sleep, work and live aboard their moving home away from home.

The Crew Only areas aboard *QM2* are extensive, discretely hidden from the passengers by unimposing 'Crew Only' signs. Crew areas serve a variety of functions. Every aspect of shipboard life needs to be taken care of. From food preparation to powering the ship, laundering sheets, towels, napkins and uniforms, to a pint after work at the Pig & Whistle (a crew bar), each activity requires its own space within *QM2*.

However, it is often the less thought about aspects of life aboard *QM2* that are most surprising. For example, the ship has a recycling plant aboard where every bottle (glass or plastic), can and milk carton is carefully sorted and stored for recycling ashore. Even more fascinating is the onboard incinerator, where the non-recyclable rubbish is disposed of in an effort to reduce the environmental burden on landfill.

Aside from the operational side of life aboard *QM2*, designers had to incorporate crew accommodation, leisure areas, bars, bathrooms and of course dining rooms (known as the Crew Mess) into the ship.

THE BRIDGE

S et high atop the ship at the forward end of the superstructure on Deck 12 is the Bridge. The hub of operations aboard the ship, the Bridge houses a central navigation area including the driving controls and a chart room, as well as a safety centre that acts as a primary response area for any incidents or emergencies at sea.

Unlike ocean liners of old, the Bridge wings aboard *QM2* are fully enclosed, allowing a greater level of comfort for the captain and officers when manoeuvring in bad weather. The enclosed nature of *QM2*'s Bridge allows for an uninterrupted span of 147.5ft from port to starboard.

DID YOU KNOW?

QM2's official signal letters are ZCEF6.

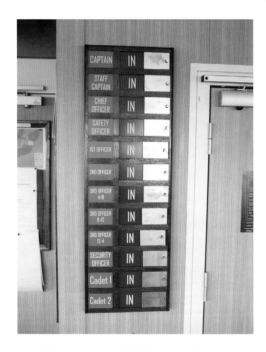

To aid in docking procedures, two large glass plates have been set into the floor of both the port and starboard Bridge Wings, allowing officers a direct view below and along the ship's side.

QM2's Bridge officers operate six watches, each lasting four hours. There is at least one senior officer, and one 3rd officer on the Bridge at all times.

Passengers can get a unique perspective on the operations of the ship from the guest viewing area. Located just aft of the Bridge and accessed via a discretely marked door on the port side of Deck 12, this area is open during selected hours on sea days.

THE GALLEY

There are ten galleys aboard *QM2* where food is prepared for the passenger restaurants, room service and for the officers and crew. As the Britannia Restaurant serves up to 1,200 people each seating, it is no surprise that the Britannia Galley is the largest aboard.

To walk through the Britannia Galley is to get a glimpse of the hard work that goes on behind the scenes to make the many fantastic dishes that passengers enjoy. The scale of the operation is overwhelming. For example, soups and stocks are prepared in giant vats, while industrial size mixers prepare batters in vast quantities.

DID YOU KNOW?

The Galley team are supported by a team of eighty-five dishwashers, pot washers and Galley cleaners – who work around the clock.

In the bakery, bread is prepared fresh daily. Loaves are baked in tins more than two times the length of a normal loaf. In the dessert department, plates are pre-prepared by the hundreds, each with decorative motifs applied with great care.

To facilitate the service to the upper levels of the Britannia Restaurant, the Britannia Galley features escalators on both the port and starboard sides, which spare the waiters' legs!

Galley	Serves
Britannia	Britannia Restaurant (up to 1,200 meals a seating)
Grills	Queens and Princess Grill (up to 400 meals a seating)
Todd English	Todd English Restaurant
La Piazza	Italian food for Kings Court
Lotus	Asian food for Kings Court
The Chef's Galley	Food prepared while you watch in the Kings Court
The Carvery	British food for Kings Court
Room Service	In-Cabin dining
Boardwalk Café	Light grill dishes and salads
Crew Galley	Catering to all the ship's officers and crew

THE STORES

With up to 4,309 passengers and crew to feed each day, it is little wonder that the *QM2*'s stores are so large. Almost all the food served aboard is prepared from scratch, using fresh ingredients stored in twenty-one refrigerated rooms. Fresh food stores are replenished every six to seven days, while dry and frozen stores are replenished every twelve to fourteen days.

The stores are serviced by the provisions team, whose job it is to load the items when the ship is in port and also to issue the stores when necessary.

While undertaking transatlantic crossings, food and beverage orders are planned three to four weeks in advance. While on longer voyages such as the World Cruise, orders are sometimes placed up to three months prior to being loaded aboard *QM2*.

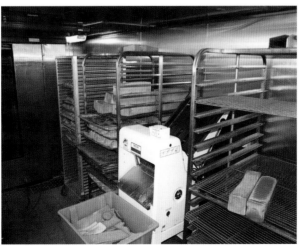

FASCINATING FOOD FACTS:

The annual sugar consumption aboard *QM2* would make eight million scones.

The *QM2* uses almost 7,000 boxes of strawberries each year.

The annual tea consumption would fill an Olympic size swimming pool.

The annual beef consumption would supply a city the size of Southampton for a year.

If you were to stack the 8,000 bags of flour used annually aboard *QM2*, the pile would be five times taller than the Eiffel Tower.

The weight of pineapples used per year is almost 90 metric tons.

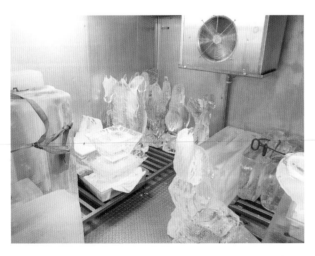

POWER PLANT

Deep in the hull of the ship you'll find the heart of *QM2*. Her primary Engine Room consists of four Wartsila W46 V1646C diesel generators, each with an output rating of 16.8MW. These giant engines are complemented by two General Electric LM2500+ gas turbines (rated at 25.0MW) which, in contrast to the diesels, reside high atop the ship within the funnel casing.

The differences between the diesel generators and the gas turbines are significant. Not only do they offer differing output but each system requires its own fuel source. While the diesels run on the more traditional maritime fuel of heavy fuel oil, the gas turbines require more refined oil known as marine gas oil. This requirement means that *QM2* takes on each of these fuels while bunkering in port.

DID YOU KNOW?

QM2 is the fastest merchant ship currently in service.

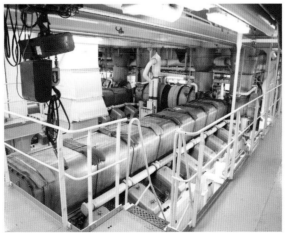

Power from the Engine Rooms provides electricity which is used for everything from powering the ship's propulsion system to lighting passenger cabins. The combination of diesels and gas turbines results in a magnificent redundancy factor whereby any combination of engines can be used to power the ship, reducing the risk of breakdowns at sea.

Both Engine Rooms are overseen by the Engine Control Room. Situated close to the primary Engine Room, the Engine Control Room is manned twenty-four hours a day in a rotation of four-hours on, eight-hours off. The ship's propulsion, powerplant (both diesel and gas) and ancillary machinery can all be managed from the Engine Control Room.

THE PODS

Below the waterline *QM2*'s propulsion system differs significantly from a traditional ocean liner. Traditional passenger ships were powered by propellers attached to propeller shafts and steered by a rudder. In contrast, *QM2* has neither of these elements.

In their place *QM2* has four Rolls Royce Mermaid pods. These pods can loosely be thought of as giant outboard motors, with the propulsion motor contained inside the pod, spinning the propeller to drive the ship.

In addition to each pod providing forward motion, the two aft pods can rotate a full 360° and act as the rudder. Each pod is rated at 21.5MW and is about the same weight as a Boeing 747 aircraft (or around 250 tons each).

DID YOU KNOW?

The pods on *QM2* pull (not push) the ship through the water – the propeller is at the front.

(Courtesy of the Warwick family collection)

CRUISING THE WORLD

Despite her primary role as a transatlantic liner, *QM2* also undertakes extensive cruising. Her cruise itineraries take her to all corners of the globe, including the Mediterranean, Northern Europe, the Baltic, the Caribbean and Canada, as well as further from home when operating the Cunard World Cruise.

Despite her relative youth, *QM2* is famous worldwide, in no small part due to her illustrious owner, the Cunard Line, as well as her immense size. She entered service as the world's largest passenger ship, earning instant fame. Ports around the world excitedly awaited their first meeting with the new Cunard Queen.

This excitement was no more evident than when, during her inaugural season in 2004, *QM2* made her maiden arrival to Hamburg, Germany. There an estimated 1 million people lined the banks of the River Elbe to welcome the ship to their city. During the same cruise she sailed on to Rotterdam where the spectacle continued with the Dutch city coming to a near stand-still.

Too large to fit through the Panama Canal, world voyages aboard *QM2* include the unique rounding of Cape Horn. *QM2*'s maiden World Cruise occurred in 2007 when she undertook an eighty-day circumnavigation of the globe. Named 'Around the World in 80 Days', the voyage included historic maiden arrivals in an array of ports including San Francisco, Auckland, Sydney, Hong Kong and Dubai.

Her fame reached new heights during this voyage when she rendezvoused with her elder sister, *QE2*, in Sydney Harbour. *QM2*, making her first call to that port, was given a royal welcome early in the morning. That evening, upon the arrival of *QE2*, everyone in Sydney, or so it seemed, stopped to watch the two Cunarders at close quarters.

Royal rendezvous between the newest Cunard Queens are now a common occurrence, providing a fantastic photo opportunity for spectators.

Representing her Country:

During the 2004 Athens Olympic Games, *QM2* operated as a Hotel Ship and played host to then French President Jacques Chirac, then British Prime Minister Tony Blair, former US President George H.W. Bush and the USA men's basketball team.

(Courtesy of Cunard Line)

THE BOSTON CUP

In a glass cabinet just aft of the Chart Room you will find the 2.5ft-tall Boston Cup. Originally known as the Britannia Cup, this two handled antique was a gift from the City of Boston to Sir Samuel Cunard. The cup took its original name from the *Britannia*, Cunard's first transatlantic liner, and it was in honour of this ship's first crossing that the cup was made.

Crafted from silver, the cup is highly decorated, with an ocean theme. On one side an image is etched of the *Britannia* at sea. On the other side is a cartouche which bears the words:

> *Presented by citizens*
> *of Boston, Mass.*
> *to the Honorable Samuel Cunard of Halifax, N.S.*
> *whose enterprise established the line of*
> *British Mail Steam Packets between*
> *Liverpool Eng.– Halifax N.S.*
> *and Boston U. States of America*
> *1840.*

The company responsible for the manufacture of the cup was Lows, Ball & Co., Boston, USA. The griffon mark of its crafter, Obidiah Rich, can be found under the base.

The cup was not ready in time for the maiden arrival of *Britannia* in 1840 and, as such, is not mentioned in the newspaper reports of the celebratory party that was held to mark the occasion. As a result, the date when it was presented to Sir Samuel Cunard is not known.

DID YOU KNOW?

The Boston Cup originally had a lid. The whereabouts of the lid remains unknown.

The cup was not documented in Cunard history and its whereabouts was unknown until 1967 when it was discovered in an antiques shop in Maryland, USA.

After Cunard took possession of the cup again it was given a place of pride on their (then) new flagship *QE2*. In 2004 the Boston Cup was symbolically transferred from *QE2* to *QM2*, thus signifying the change of flagship for the Cunard Line and creating a tradition.

DID YOU KNOW?

QM2 is more than five times longer than Cunard's first ship, *Britannia*.

THE MASTER'S PERSPECTIVE

BY COMMODORE BERNARD WARNER

As I mix with our guests on board, there are two questions which I frequently get asked:

1) 'If you're here who is driving?' and
2) 'What is a commodore?'

In actual fact commodore means the senior captain in the fleet, but I fulfil the same role as the captain on board in that I am the master of the ship.

I felt both fortunate and privileged to be appointed master of *Queen Mary 2* in the summer of 2005. Having spent most of my career with P&O, it had never really crossed my mind that I might have the opportunity to one day command the most famous and greatest ocean liner in the world.

Queen Mary 2 is a liner because she maintains a regular summer service across the North Atlantic Ocean. After being christened by Her Majesty Queen Elizabeth II on 8 January 2004, *Queen Mary 2* took over the Cunard transatlantic service from *Queen Elizabeth 2*, and we are now the only ship providing regular Atlantic crossings. As well as these transatlantic crossings, we have a wide and varied itinerary; from world cruises to much shorter voyages throughout Europe, the Caribbean and North America.

Queen Mary 2 has been specially strengthened to perform well in all weather conditions. She was designed with a long sleek bow, deep draught and a beautifully streamlined hull, enabling her to slip gracefully through the water. Efficient Rolls Royce fin stabilisers dampen the roll of the ship and, without doubt, this ship moves less than any other liner or cruise ship afloat. Although 'moves less' may be the wrong choice of words because she can actually achieve a full speed of 29.5 knots. So, besides being extremely stable, she can outrun all the opposition as well!

As commodore, my primary responsibility is for the safe navigation of *Queen Mary 2* and the well being of all the guests and crew on board. The crew is the lifeblood of our ship, and they make *Queen Mary 2* the success that she truly is. Their hard work and pride in our ship sets us apart from the competition in terms of comfort, service, fine dining and entertainment.

Queen Mary 2's interior features are like no other ship. Because it was decided she would not use the Panama Canal, she is a very wide and long ship, which allows exciting spaces for our guests.

After dining in the spectacular Britannia Restaurant, you might wish to take a novel from the elegant 8,000 book library and relax in the Winter Garden. Follow this with a work out in the gym and then a brisk walk around the Promenade Deck and into the Canyon Ranch Spaclub for a richly deserved pampering.

In Illuminations *Queen Mary 2* boasts the first planetarium at sea which can also double as a lecture theatre and cinema. The Cunard Insights programme offers something for everyone. We tend to offer guests more than just lectures, and they are able to interact with the experts, many of them famous, in fields such as show business, exploration, oceanography, politics, finance, history and sport.

The ConneXions conference centre features abundant space for conducting business at sea, with more meeting facilities than any other ship. Over 78 per cent of staterooms have balconies, and our staterooms vary from a sizeable 18m² all the way up to the Grand Duplex of 209m².

The West End Stage is brought to life in the Royal Court Theatre with dynamic musicals and celebrity entertainers, and one of the special features of our ship is the Queens Room. It has the largest dance floor at sea and provides ever popular big band dancing throughout the voyage. There is a feeling of space and luxury everywhere you walk!

The ship is filled with memorabilia depicting past great liners and the famous that have travelled with Cunard. Our guests can follow the Maritime Quest which relates in audio the history of the company from Samuel Cunard's first transatlantic with *Britannia* in 1840 through to the present day.

I had the pleasure of being aboard while Chris and Rachelle researched this book. Their pictures capture the true splendour of *Queen Mary 2* and I recommend this book to all those that love ships and the sea.

Now that you have toured the ship we hope that you will join us one day and experience all the delights of this beautiful ocean liner.

Commodore Bernard Warner

Master - *Queen Mary 2*

2009

AFTERWORD

BY COMMODORE RYND

Following my appointment as the new Commodore of the Cunard Fleet, and my return to the *Queen Mary 2*, I am impressed anew by this truly unique vessel.

True to the liner tradition she offers one of the world's great journeys, the transatlantic crossing. She does this in the style and elegance of her predecessors, but in greater comfort. She also carries out seasonal short voyages and annual world voyages.

This is a magnificent vessel and forms a link between North America and Europe with her regularly scheduled crossings. She complements the great ports she visits and they in turn are complemented by her presence in a way no other merchant vessel can do.

This book, *QM2: A Photographic Journey* captures well, in both pictures and words, what makes this vessel unique and illustrates why she attracts such a loyal following, from both her passengers and crew.

Christopher Rynd
Commodore, Cunard Line
Master, *Queen Mary 2*

DID YOU KNOW?

QM2 is the only ocean liner currently offering scheduled transatlantic crossings.

QM2 FACTS

GENERAL INFORMATION

Name:	*Queen Mary 2 (QM2)*
Gross registered tonnage:	151,400 tons
Passenger decks:	13 (Plus 3L)
Length:	1,132ft (345m)
Width:	135ft (40m)
Width at Bridge Wings:	147.5ft (45m)
Draft:	32ft 10in (10m)
Height (Keel to Funnel):	236.2ft (72m)
Builders:	Chantiers de l'Atlantique, France
Keel laid:	4 July 2002
Floating out date:	21 March 2003
Maiden voyage:	12 January 2004
Maximum passenger capacity:	3,056
Standard crew capacity:	1,253
Port of registry:	Hamilton, Bermuda
Official number and signal letters:	9241061 and ZCEF6
Owners:	Cunard Line

ENGINE ROOM INFORMATION

Diesel engines:	Four 16-cylinder Wartsila 'V engines'
Gas Turbines:	Two General Electric LM25s00+ gas turbines
Power:	157,000hp
Propulsion system:	Four pods of 20MW each. Two fixed and two azimuth
Bow thrusters:	Three 3.2MW thrusters
Stabilizers:	Four VM Series Stabilizers at 70 tons each
Anchors:	Three 23-ton anchors – two working and one spare
Anchor chains:	Three anchor chains; collectively 843 yards (771m) long
Ship building cost:	Approximately US$800 million

INTERESTING FACTS

Inside QM2 there are...

2,500km (1,553 miles) of electric cable

500km (310 miles) of ducts, mains and pipes

2,000 bathrooms

80,000 lighting points

250,000sq.m (280,000 square yards) of fitted carpets

120,000sq.m (144,000 square yards) of insulating material

3,200sq.m (3,800 square yards) of galleys

3,000 telephones

8,800 loudspeakers

5,000 stairs

5,000 fire detectors

1,100 fire doors

8,350 automatic extinguishers

BIBLIOGRAPHY

Braynard, F.O and Miller, W.H. (1991), *Picture History of the Cunard Line* (Dover, United Kingdom).

Gandy, M. (1982), *The Antiques Magazine*, The Britannia Cup (July '82 edition), Volume 122. pp. 156-158.

Grant, R.G. (2007), *Flight: The Complete History* (Dorling Kindersley Ltd, United Kingdom).

Maxtone-Graham, J. and Lloyd, H. (2004), *Queen Mary 2: The Greatest Ocean Liner of Our Time* (Bulfinch, United Kingdom).

Miller, W.H. (2001), *Picture History of British Ocean Liners: 1900 to the Present* (Dover, United Kingdom).

Miller, W.H. (1995), *Pictorial Encyclopedia of Ocean Liners 1860-1994* (Dover. United Kingdom).

Plisson, P. (2004), *Queen Mary 2: The Birth of a Legend* (Harry. N. Abrams. United Kingdom).

Cunard Line (2009), *Onboard Promotional Material* (Various Versions).

Cunard Line (2009), *Queen Mary 2: Technical and Bridge Facts* (Various Versions).

Personal Conversations:

Commodore R.W. Warwick
Commodore B. Warner
Captain N. Bates
Chief Engineer B. Wattling
Food & Beverage Manager S. Engl
Marine Supervisor A. Gould
1st Officer D. Hudson
2nd Officer S. Roje
3rd Officer H. Johnson
3rd Officer C. Wood
Deck Cadet H. Morley
Captain's Secretary C. Hansen
Technical Secretary E. Wealleans
Cunard Line PR Executive M. Gallagher

Websites:

Chris' Cunard Page: http://www.chriscunard.com/
Cunard's Official UK Homepage: http://www.cunard.co.uk/
Cunard's Official US Homepage: http://www.cunard.com/
Sam Warwick's *QM2* Homepage: http://www.QM2.org.uk/

Stay in Touch with the Authors:

(Twitter Logo) @chriscunard
(Facebook logo) facebook.com/chriscunard
(Instragram Logo) @chriscunard
(youTube logo) youtube.com/chriscunard
(Flickr Logo) flickr.com/chriscunard

QM2 from the Rock of Gibraltar. (Courtesy of Andy Fitzsimmons)

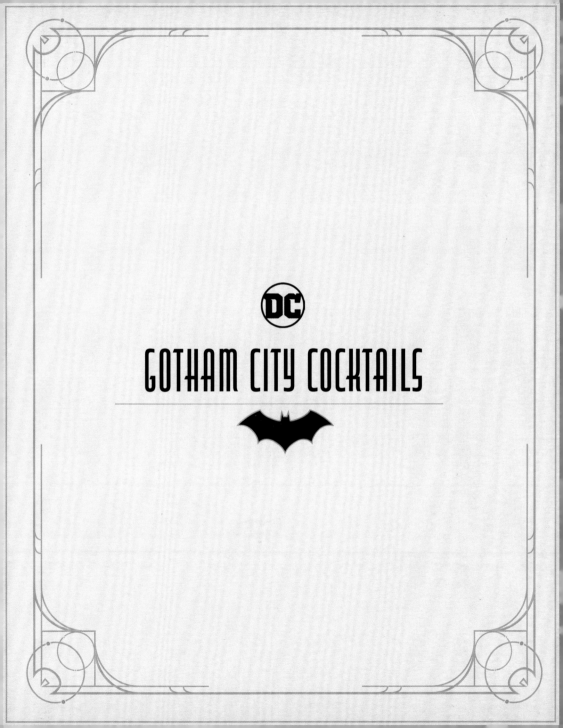

GOTHAM CITY COCKTAILS

GOTHAM CITY COCKTAILS

OFFICIAL HANDCRAFTED FOOD & DRINKS FROM THE WORLD OF BATMAN

70 RECIPES INSPIRED BY THE HOMETOWN OF DC'S ICONIC SUPER HERO

WRITTEN BY ANDRÉ DARLINGTON

PHOTOGRAPHS BY TED THOMAS

INSIGHT
EDITIONS

San Rafael • Los Angeles • London

TO THE THIRSTY CITIZENS OF GOTHAM CITY

CONTENTS

A BRIEF HISTORY OF
GOTHAM CITY COCKTAILS

Hear that? It's the clink of ice in a shaker, the clatter of glass smashing to the ground. On every corner in Gotham City, you'll find gilded hotel bars, modern cocktail dens, and cozy speakeasies. This is a city with a rich and varied nightlife, and the cocktail options never end. Tumble down a back-alley staircase into a basement joint, or ride an elevator up to the top of a skyscraper into a private club—you'll find something to slake your thirst. Plus, it's a hell of a place to drink; you never know who's going to come swinging through the door.

Gotham City was built by big personalities and has been shaped by epic events. Its mixed drinks are similarly legendary. The town's famous cocktails have been created by bartenders who have lived it—the triumphs and the tragedies—and have shaken and stirred for the good guys as well as the bad. The city's great bartenders have commemorated Gotham City life in liquid form, and they have passed along their recipes to us. We have them to thank for the classics of Park Row's heyday and the faddish drinks inspired by entertainers like the Flying Graysons.

There are a few things for the uninitiated to know about Gotham City's unique mixed drinks. Like other important ports on the Eastern Seaboard, the first cocktails were based on rum. After independence, the preferred spirit became rye whiskey. But it was during Prohibition when things really started to get interesting, when Gotham City diverged from everywhere else. Bars, especially those in the Narrows, never closed. Business boomed as out-of-towners flocked to the city. Because of this legacy, Gotham City's cocktails are a little stronger, a little stranger, a little . . . darker.

Today, the craft cocktail craze that has swept the nation has arrived in Gotham City. There is a renewed interest in mixed drinks, and a new generation of enthusiasts have sleuthed out lost recipes and reformulated old ones for modern tastes. The cocktails collected here come from newspaper and magazine clippings, bartender interviews, private club records, and some old-school detective work. Sadly, many once-famous drinks have been lost to us. But we've rediscovered a lot, and they are all here to enjoy.

This collection of Gotham City's essential cocktails will guide you as you create your home bar inspired by the home of the Caped Crusader—what to drink, essential ingredients and tools to add to your Utility Belt, and step-by-step instructions for easily crafting these enticing recipes. By shaking and stirring these epic cocktails, you can join in celebrating this town's great characters and signature landmarks. Gotham City is a mysterious and beloved place, and the drinks gathered here bring us one step closer to understanding what makes this town tick. Got a big thirst, fast pulse, and a clever retort? This book is for you.

HOW TO USE THIS BOOK

The cocktails in this book are divided into sections based on occasion as well as manner of manufacture. This is to assist you with finding drinks that fit your tastes and needs. The first section is composed of lighter fare—versions of champagne cocktails, highballs, and spritzes—drinks that are great party starters or easy sippers. Next up are built cocktails, such as riffs on the old-fashioned and the mojito, that are muddled or have other in-glass techniques, followed by shaken drinks, such as daiquiris, and then a section on stirred drinks, such as martinis and Manhattans. If you are looking for large-format cocktails—punches, teas, party bowls—head to the fifth chapter: One Punch. Finally, Night to Day is where to find morning drinks like the Bloody Mary and salty dog—as well as after-dinner drinks like an espresso martini. Cocktails are organized alphabetically within each chapter.

The seventh chapter is a collection of essential and delicious Gotham City small bites, including an excellent crab rémoulade recipe by well-known philanthropist Martha Wayne, and Wayne Manor mulligatawny soup by Alfred Pennyworth, personal butler to the Wayne family and famous for his expertise at crafting food for events. At the end of the book, you will find information regarding items necessary for a well-stocked cocktail pantry, valuable technique tips, and additional resources for the avid cocktailer.

EQUIPMENT CHECKLIST

Crafting great cocktails does not require many fancy or expensive gadgets, but there are a few items that make mixing drinks easier and improves their quality. For more information on cocktail pantry items and techniques, see page 134.

BARSPOON

A barspoon is a great help for making properly stirred cocktails, as well as measuring ingredients. One with enough heft at the end of the handle to crack ice is best. Barspoons are widely available in kitchen stores and online.

BOSTON SHAKER

The classic three-part shaker, often called a martini shaker, is not suitable for making most cocktails, and the lid tends to stick. The preferred piece of equipment for modern bartenders is the two-part Boston shaker. Originally it was composed of a metal tin and a glass pint cup, but today the two parts are both metal. This prevents breakage if the glass slips from your hands. These two-part metal shakers are now widely available in kitchen stores and online.

CITRUS PRESS

Hand juicers work for small amounts of liquid, but it is good to have a larger one with a reservoir when juicing a lot of citrus. It may be worth investing in a quality juicer if you are making drinks frequently.

GLASSWARE

No special glassware is required to enjoy a good cocktail. However, note that the average drink sizes for proper cocktails are small when poured into most common commercial glassware. Many big-box stores sell oversize glassware that is not suitable for today's craft cocktails. If you prefer cocktail-specific glasses, your first choice may be to invest in a set of coupe glasses—sometimes called champagne glasses—which are now widely available online. The best size for these is between four and six ounces. Additionally, good highball and rocks glasses can enhance presentation. The glassware mentioned in the recipes for this book are cocktail glass, or coupe glass; rocks glass, or tumbler; highball glass, or tall cylinder; plus shot glass, julep cup, wineglass, champagne flute, and hip flask.

JIGGER

Measuring precisely is a must for quality drinks. The standard unit of measure for cocktail mixing is ounces. You can find jiggers ranging in size from 0.5 to 2.5 ounces.

MIXING GLASS

Mixing glasses are used for all stirred drinks, including Manhattans, Negronis, martinis, and many more. Glasses have come down in price in the past few years and are recommended in order to make stirred drinks correctly.

MUDDLER

Anything blunt can be used to muddle, but a real cocktail muddler makes the work a snap. A muddler should be constructed of nonstained, nonreactive wood. Steer clear of plastic, metal, or painted ones.

STRAINERS

There are two main styles of cocktail strainers: Hawthorne and julep. Typically, Hawthorne strainers are used for shaken drinks, while julep strainers are used for stirred cocktails. If you are in doubt, buy a Hawthorne, which works fine for both purposes.

Y-PEELER

A Y-peeler, sometimes called a Swiss peeler, is the best piece of equipment for creating citrus peel garnishes. It is an inexpensive and useful kitchen tool.

OTHER HELPFUL ITEMS TO CONSIDER

- Bottle opener
- Cocktail picks
- Cutting board
- Funnel
- Hand towels
- Ice bucket
- Ice scoop
- Large-format ice cube trays
- Microplane
- Paring knife
- Squeeze bottles (for citrus juice)
- Wine key corkscrew

STEMLESS WINEGLASS

MIXING GLASS AND ROCKS GLASS

COUPE GLASS

HIGHBALL GLASS

FLUTE

MARTINI GLASS

SHOT GLASS

· ORIGINS ·
STARTER COCKTAILS

The cocktails in this chapter are ideal for beginning your evening or whiling away afternoons. They also require the least effort because you can simply pour and enjoy! But just because they are a snap doesn't mean these aren't some of the best and most important drinks in Gotham City; in fact, because they are easy and relatively light, they are often the most popular kind of cocktail. Expect everything from a secret mix inspired by the ever-prepared Alfred Pennyworth to popular gala drinks every socialite in town knows. Note that while champagne is ideal, the drinks in this chapter requiring bubbly can be made with crémant or a high-quality dry prosecco.

THE
DARK NIGHTCAP

Every cocktailer in Gotham City knows this brooding drink, which is a favorite at bars and restaurants. Amaro is the dark cloak of the spirits world. Here, it wraps around scotch to make a highball of great mystery and depth, while bitters add the knockout punch. No matter what catastrophes befall Gotham City, Batman will always be there to save the day—much like this drink. There is no better cocktail with which to toast the Dark Knight.

1½ ounce blended scotch

1 ounce Averna

2 ounces club soda

2 dashes Angostura bitters, for garnish

Lemon peel, for garnish

Combine scotch, Averna, and soda in a rocks glass with ice.
Stir, and top with bitters. Garnish with a lemon peel.

THE
BURNSIDER

Young, worldly, and tech-savvy, the new residents of Gotham City's exploding Burnside neighborhood are ultrahip. The best local bars and restaurants have taken note of this influx and created a number of drinks for a cohort who wants to hang out with friends but still get back to work later. The most famous of these smart concoctions is called, appropriately enough, the Burnsider—low in alcohol but high in glam and flavor. It's the signature cocktail for a neighborhood that includes newsworthy movers and shakers like Barbara Gordon.

5 ounces ginger beer

½ ounce Cointreau

¼ ounce fresh lemon juice

Lemon peel, for garnish

Combine the ginger beer, Cointreau, and lemon juice in a champagne flute, and stir gently. Garnish with a lemon peel.

THE
BUTLER

Other than acknowledging that he grew up in England, Alfred Pennyworth
rarely mentions his life before Wayne Manor. What is certain is Alfred's
impeccable taste, no doubt shaped by his travels around the world outside
Wayne Manor. Although the gin and tonic originated in India among the
British soldiers stationed there—the quinine once in tonic prevented
malaria—this version is decidedly Southeast Asian–inspired. Makrut lime
leaves impart a bright flavor that is a great accompaniment to grilled meats.
The leaves are readily available in Asian grocery stores and freeze well for
later use.

1 makrut lime leaf

4 whole black peppercorns

1 lemon peel

2½ ounces gin

4 ounces tonic water

Cucumber slice, for garnish

**Fill a highball glass or wineglass to the top with ice.
Add the lime leaf, peppercorns, and lemon peel. Top with the gin and
tonic water, and stir gently. Garnish with a cucumber slice.**

GOOD VS. EVIL

Batman and The Joker are locked in a struggle between order and chaos. Theirs is a battle for the ages, each balancing out the other as they wage war over Gotham City. The rum and ginger beer in this cocktail exist side by side with a similar epic tension. But give it the slightest stir, and the harmony disappears into a confrontation of flavors. Note that the Benedictine can be omitted, but it adds a nuttiness that gives this drink a unique taste.

4 ounces ginger beer

1 ounce dark rum

½ ounce Benedictine (optional)

Lime wheel, for garnish

Fill a highball glass with ice, and add the ginger beer. Add the rum and Benedictine, and garnish with a lime wheel. Stir and watch the colors blend together.

FULL DECK

The Joker loves to crash parties. He loves to crash, blast, slam, and wham parties. Much like the Clown Prince of Crime, this riotous cocktail is purple and green and sets the room spinning. This concoction is the perfect way to kick off festivities and start feeling funny. But beware, if you have too many, *you* won't be playing with a full deck, either. Why not accessorize? Add a green spiral straw to complete the look.

½ ounce crème de violette

4 ounces champagne

Cucumber spiral, for garnish

Pour the crème de violette and champagne into a champagne flute, stir, and garnish with a cucumber spiral. Serve with a green spiral straw.

FELINE FATALE

The most famous classic spritzes are a mix of prosecco, club soda, and either Aperol or Campari—these are colorful, bitter aperitifs that taste like grapefruit and orange. Spritzes can also be made with an amaro such as Cynar or Montenegro. However, if you are looking for a little purr in your spritz, elderflower liqueur is the nimble addition. All felines seem to agree on a blend of half elderflower and half Campari.

1 ounce elderflower liqueur

1 ounce Campari

2 ounces prosecco

1 ounce club soda

Lemon slice, for garnish

Combine the elderflower liqueur, Campari, prosecco, and club soda in a wineglass with ice, and stir. Garnish with a lemon slice, and serve with a straw.

GOTHAM CITY ROYAL

A champagne cocktail is a sure way to get any party off to a successful start. Classy, glam, and a little naughty, this version with all-American whiskey is a hit in Gotham City. Think of this as a perfect drink for toasting special occasions, whether a gala or a romantic dinner. As the sugar cube dissolves, it makes a stream of bubbles—putting on quite a show as you sip. Guests will love the drink's fascinating appearance as well as the added whiskey oomph.

1 sugar cube

1 barspoon orange bitters

½ ounce bourbon

4 ounces champagne

1 orange peel

Drop the sugar cube into the bottom of a champagne flute, and wet with the orange bitters. Add the bourbon, and top with the champagne. Twist the orange peel over the glass to express the oils in the rind, and discard.

THE
COMMISSIONER

A collins is a drink that includes liquor, lemon juice, sugar, and club soda. The format was once so popular that it spawned its own type of glassware—the collins glass. These are similar to highball glasses, except taller. The most famous collins versions employ gin, but this is a mixed drink that is open to variation. A steadfast and bona fide classic, the added scotch imparts a depth and gravitas befitting a dedicated officer of the law like Commissioner James Gordon.

2 ounces blended scotch

¾ ounce fresh lemon juice

½ ounce Simple Syrup (page 137)

2 ounces club soda

Lemon peel, for garnish

Combine the scotch, lemon juice, and Simple Syrup with ice in a highball glass. Stir, and top with the club soda. Garnish with a lemon peel.

LUCKY PENNY

This cocktail has been a Gotham City favorite thanks to its bright and refreshing profile. The chief ingredient here is Pimm's, a signature British liqueur that tastes wonderfully citrusy with subtle spice notes. Its most famous application is in a Pimm's Cup—this is an easy variation of that venerable drink. The Lucky Penny is a party favorite, and it is a perfect match for seafood but also works well at brunch with toast and marmalade.

2 ounces Pimm's No. 1 (or substitute 1 part gin,
1 part red vermouth, and ½ part curaçao)

4 ounces ginger beer

½ ounce fresh lemon juice

Fresh mint sprig, for garnish

Combine the Pimm's No. 1, ginger beer, and lemon juice in a highball glass filled with ice, and stir. Garnish with a mint sprig.

ELEGY

The famous, rich, and beautiful Kathy Kane spends her time flitting from shopping sprees to parties and making headlines in the gossip sections of magazines. This low-proof cocktail is a chic number that will help you always keep your wits as she does—with a healthy splash of pizzazz from pomegranate. It is the perfect accessory for a busy social life. Combining two types of vermouth, also known as splitting, is a clever way to add complex flavor to a mixed drink, but choosing one is just fine, too.

1½ ounces dry vermouth

1 ounce blanc vermouth

½ ounce pomegranate juice

3 ounces club soda

Lemon twist, for garnish

Combine the vermouths, pomegranate juice, and club soda with ice in a highball glass, and stir. Garnish with a lemon twist.

BUILT COCKTAILS

Cocktails that require a little handiwork in the glass are a peculiar species, rather rare compared with other styles of mixed-drink manufacture such as shaking and stirring. But these are enormously important drinks, rightfully famous both for their flavor and for the ritual involved. Note that in the cocktail world, *built* often means simply poured into the glass. Here we mean drinks that are muddled or in some way constructed. A few famous cocktails that fall into this category are old-fashioneds (called Old Gothams in Gotham City) as well as Sazeracs, mojitos, and juleps. These are drinks that require a muddler and are made by preparing a glass with sugar, fruit, or herbs. The extra effort is always worth it, imparting both pageantry and depth of flavor to the resulting drink.

OLD GOTHAM

This was the first recipe to combine the four ingredients necessary to be deemed a proper cocktail: spirit, bitters, sugar, and water (ice). Today, the Old Gotham is often made with whiskey, but originally it would have been prepared with rum from Gotham City's many distilleries. The use of candied orange peel is a bit of a mystery; it is likely oranges were brought to the city by pirate ships plying the waters off Gotham City in the late eighteenth century. The addition is magical and is still found in all the city's best hotel bars and steak houses. During the Depression, there was a shortage of sugar cubes, and the city's bartenders muddled the candied orange peel in the bottom of the glass. This is a great variation on the drink, which is still found at bars in the Narrows.

The manufacture of the Old Gotham is unique among cocktails. It begins with a sugar cube moistened with bitters and a splash of water. Be sure to completely muddle the sugar and smear it around the bottom of the glass until it begins to dissolve.

1 sugar cube

2 dashes Angostura bitters

1 teaspoon water

2 ounces rum

Candied orange peel, for garnish

Lemon twist, for garnish

Muddle the sugar cube, Angostura bitters, and water in a rocks glass. Add ice and the rum. Garnish with a candied orange peel and lemon twist.

THE
DEMON'S HEAD

The English translation of Rā's al Ghūl is *head of the demon*, and this cocktail captures the man's pure evil in a very dramatic way. Butterfly pea flowers have been used for centuries in tea, and their deep blue petals make a natural dye. One of the flower's distinctive features in liquid form is that it changes color based on the pH of substances added to it—for instance, lime juice. Watch in amazement as the color of this drink transforms from blue to purple. It is an impressive trick that Gotham City's bartenders use to wow guests. Note that butterfly pea flower powder and liquid are available online.

2 ounces vodka

1 barspoon butterfly pea flower liquid

¾ ounce fresh lime juice

1 ounce Cointreau

Combine the vodka and butterfly pea flower liquid in an ice-filled rocks glass. Shake the lime juice and Cointreau with ice, and strain slowly into the rocks glass.

CAPE & COWL

This cocktail began as a joke. It became popular when Batman first appeared and was intended to make fun of the new vigilante dressed as a bat. Legend has it a colorful bartender with a twisted sense of humor thought it would be hilarious to mix cucumber and whiskey. While unusual, the surprising combination works well, and these days, the cocktail is such a crowd-pleaser that bartenders pre-batch it to keep up with demand. Originally, it was muddled according to the recipe below.

1 cucumber slice

1 barspoon Simple Syrup (page 137)

1 dash Peychaud's bitters

1½ ounces bourbon

¾ ounce dry vermouth

¼ ounce Fernet Branca

Fresh mint sprig, for garnish

Muddle the cucumber in a mixing glass with the Simple Syrup and Peychaud's bitters. Add the whiskey, vermouth, and Fernet Branca. Fill the mixing glass with ice, and stir. Strain into a chilled rocks glass, and garnish with a mint sprig.

THE NARROWS ORIGINAL

The Narrows has long been associated with poverty and crime. It is hard to imagine that once it was a wealthy bedroom community for Gotham City's finance men. During this gilded age, there were a number of elegant bars, and the area's most famous libation is named for the neighborhood. This is a very strong drink—all liquor—employing absinthe and also applejack, one of Gotham City's early favorite spirits. The Narrows is also unique for its two-glass method of manufacture.

¼ ounce absinthe

1 sugar cube

1 dash Angostura bitters

2 ounces rye whiskey

¼ ounce Laird's applejack

Lemon peel

Fill a rocks glass with ice, and add the absinthe. Place the sugar cube in a second glass, and wet the cube with the Angostura bitters. Crush the sugar with a muddler or barspoon, and add the whiskey and applejack. Add ice, and stir. Empty the ice from the prepared first glass, and strain the whiskey mixture into it. Twist a lemon peel to express the oil over the glass, and discard.

SUIT UP

Sometimes dinner is just the beginning of the night. For all those who need a boost with classic digestif favorites—such as whiskey and amaro—this Gotham City classic is a lifesaver. It is a clever brew, adding just enough strong coffee to make a balanced cocktail that doesn't reveal its caffeine payload. This perfect pick-me-up is often ordered from a knowing bartender or server with a simple nod of the head following a meal.

1 sugar cube

2 dashes Angostura bitters

1 ounce rye whiskey

1 ounce cold coffee

½ ounce amaro

Lemon twist, for garnish

Muddle the sugar and Angostura bitters in a rocks glass until the sugar dissolves. Fill the glass with ice. Add the whiskey, coffee, and amaro, and stir until combined. Garnish with a lemon twist.

PEÑA DURO

Peña Duro is the infamous prison where Bane was incarcerated. One of Batman's most vicious adversaries, Bane is said to have escaped from the hellish facility to become one of Gotham City's most notorious criminals. Peña Duro is located on the Caribbean island of Santa Prisca, birthplace of a number of well-known warm-weather cocktails. But of all the island's drinks, this is its most famous. It is hugely popular in Gotham City, particularly during the summer months.

½ lime, cut into 4 wedges

1 barspoon granulated sugar

4 fresh mint leaves

1 ounce white rum

1 ounce overproof rum

1 ounce club soda

Muddle 3 of the lime wedges with the sugar in a rocks glass.
Add the mint leaves, and muddle gently. Add the rums and ice, and stir.
Top with the club soda, and garnish with the remaining lime wedge.

THE
TAIL FIN

The Batmobile is the single greatest piece of equipment prowling the streets of Gotham City. While it's the cause of some anxiety, the beast is also a source of great pride for the city's residents. A few cocktails have been created over the years to glorify this impressive vehicle, but none is as famous as the Tail Fin. The cobbled ice in the drink represents the streets of Gotham City, and the two cherries resemble the car's taillights—which are all most people ever see.

3 fresh mint leaves, plus mint sprig, for garnish

1 ounce rye whiskey

1 ounce Campari

¾ ounce sweet vermouth

½ ounce dry vermouth

1 dash Benedictine (optional)

2 Amarena cherries

Muddle the mint leaves in a rocks glass or julep cup, and top with crushed ice. Pour the whiskey, Camparai, vermouths, and Benedictine, if using, over the ice, and stir until the glass is cold. Garnish with a mint sprig and cherries on a cocktail pick. Serve with a straw.

· IN THE MIX ·
SHAKEN COCKTAILS

As a general rule, cocktails are shaken when they include citrus, eggs, or dairy. Shaking properly emulsifies and aerates the drink. This style of manufacture means that, in this chapter, you will find sours like variations on daiquiris and margaritas along with luscious cream or egg drinks like flips. Contrary to popular belief, the martini—because it is a spirits-only cocktail—is not shaken, so it does not appear here. You can find more on the reason for this on page 137. Because the most common shaken drinks contain citrus, the cocktails in this chapter are refreshing and typically lower in ABV (alcohol by volume) than their stirred cousins.

BATARANG

MAKES 2 SERVINGS

The Batarang is a nonlethal, multifunctional tool that Batman uses in his crusade for justice. Gotham City bartenders took this as inspiration for a style of shot they secretly send to one another via courier while they are on shift. The receiving party then sends the same drink, or a similar one, back. Think of it as a liquid high-five, a vital drink for Gotham City bartenders to have in their arsenals.

3 fresh mint leaves

1 ounce gin

1 ounce blended scotch

½ ounce fresh lemon juice

½ ounce Simple Syrup (page 137)

1 dash orange bitters

Shake the mint leaves, gin, scotch, lemon juice, Simple Syrup, and orange bitters with ice, and strain into shot glasses.

DIAMOND THIEF

Rumor has it the first time Batman met Catwoman, she was a mysterious burglar engaged in stealing a valuable necklace. Right from the start, she both antagonized and attracted Batman. This classic Prohibition-era Gotham City gem is a heady mix of rum and sweet vermouth with added fruit juice—so delicious it may prompt a heist. The pineapple gives the drink a thrillingly frothy texture, as light as a thief's touch.

1½ ounces white rum

1 ounce sweet vermouth

¼ ounce maraschino liqueur

¼ ounce fresh lime juice

1½ ounces fresh pineapple juice

1 dash Angostura bitters

Pineapple wedge, for garnish

Shake the rum, vermouth, maraschino liqueur, lime juice, pineapple juice, and Angostura bitters with ice, and strain into a cocktail glass. Garnish with a pineapple wedge.

COLD CASE

Renee Montoya is a detective in the Major Crimes Unit of the Gotham
City Police Department. It is a position she achieved in record time—
and this should be no surprise to anyone because she graduated at the
top of her class. Montoya is an extraordinarily dedicated second-generation
immigrant whose parents came from the Dominican Republic.
Passion fruit is widely grown there, and its tart flavor makes
for one of the world's great daiquiri variations.

1½ ounces light rum

1½ ounces passion fruit juice

¾ ounce fresh lime juice

¼ ounce Simple Syrup (page 137)

Lime wheel, for garnish

**Shake the rum, passion fruit juice, lime juice, and Simple Syrup with ice,
and strain into a cocktail glass. Garnish with a lime wheel.**

FLIP OF A COIN

Unable to make a clear decision on his own, Two-Face relies on the flip of his coin to determine his courses of action. One side of his coin is unblemished, the other is deeply scarred—the side that turns up decides which of his personalities will win. Two-Face was an easy target for Gotham City's bartenders, and they set to work creating a number of popular flips when he began appearing in news headlines. Reward yourself with the amazing froth and luscious consistency of this winning drink.

2 ounces whiskey

½ ounce Cointreau

½ ounce fresh lemon juice

1 egg

1 teaspoon superfine sugar

Freshly grated nutmeg, for garnish

Shake the whiskey, Cointreau, lemon juice, egg, and sugar vigorously with ice, and strain into a cocktail glass. Garnish with nutmeg.

NO SAFETY NET

The Flying Graysons were one of Gotham City's most illustrious entertaining groups. A family of trapeze artists who, for added drama, worked without a net, they became an overnight sensation. This cocktail appeared in Gotham City shortly after their rise to fame and is notable for containing crème de violette—a blue-purple liqueur that represents the sky. Crème de violette is also used in the classic Aviation cocktail. The three cherries represent the family on the high wire.

2 ounces white rum

¾ ounce fresh lemon juice

½ ounce maraschino liqueur

¼ ounce crème de violette

3 cherries

Shake the rum, lemon juice, maraschino liqueur, and crème de violette with ice, and strain into a cocktail glass. Garnish with the cherries on a cocktail pick resting across the top of the glass.

KING OF FEAR

The villain Scarecrow is famous for using experimental toxins in order to exploit the deep-seated fears of his victims. He purportedly wears a face mask that makes him look like the decoys farmers employ to discourage birds from eating crops before harvest—hence this cocktail features a full array of fall flavors. This is an especially popular drink in Gotham City around Halloween, but it's appropriate whenever the weather turns cold. Enjoy with a hearty meal and a spine-chilling ghost story.

1½ ounces blended scotch

1 ounce Averna or Montenegro

1 ounce fresh pineapple juice

¼ ounce Simple Syrup (page 137)

1 dash Angostura bitters

Pumpkin pie spice, for garnish

Shake the scotch, Averna (or Montenegro), pineapple juice, Simple Syrup, and Angostura bitters with ice, and strain into a rocks glass with ice. Garnish with pumpkin pie spice.

THE
LAST LAUGH

It is curious how many super-villains like to get the last laugh—
but don't we all? This crazy-delicious cocktail was adapted by Gotham City
bartenders from a pre-Prohibition drink called the Last Word and features an
uproarious mix of herbaceous mezcal and complex green Chartreuse. This is
now a classic, sporting an amusing green color as well as a riotous flavor.

¼ ounce absinthe

¾ ounce mezcal

¾ ounce green Chartreuse

¾ ounce maraschino liqueur

¾ ounce fresh lemon juice

Lime wheel, for garnish

Rinse a cocktail glass with the absinthe. Shake the mezcal,
Chartreuse, maraschino liqueur, and lemon juice with ice, and strain
into a cocktail glass. Garnish with a lime wheel.

THE
CRUSADER

Fearless adventurers have a long history in film, inspiring courage and derring-do in all of us. We like to believe we might be capable of the same feats. This enlivening mix is a salute to every swashbuckler who seeks justice—making it a popular pre-theater cocktail in Gotham City. Apricot brandy was once a trendy ingredient among the jet-set actors who played big Hollywood movie roles; during Prohibition, local apricots were used to make liquor, which is why it appears in so many cocktails from that great era.

1 egg white (from a medium egg)

1½ ounces gin

1 ounce apricot brandy

½ ounce fresh lemon juice

1 dash Peychaud's bitters (optional)

Shake the egg white, gin, brandy, and lemon juice vigorously with ice, and strain into a cocktail glass. Garnish with the Peychaud's bitters, if desired.

ALTER EGO

This cocktail is a favorite at the bar My Alibi, which you might know as the spot Two-Face visited after escaping Arkham Asylum. The bartenders there make it when any customer is in a "mood." Amer Picon can be difficult to source but is easily replaced by China-China, an additional orange-flavored liqueur with a similar taste. Alternatively, you can add another one-fourth ounce maraschino liqueur and skip the orange liqueur altogether. Whiskey and grapefruit juice are a classic winning combination—a useful pair for creating your own mixed drinks.

2 ounces rye whiskey

1 ounce fresh grapefruit juice

¼ ounce maraschino liqueur

**¼ ounce Amer Picon
(substitute China-China or maraschino liqueur)**

Grapefruit twist, for garnish

Shake the whiskey, grapefruit juice, maraschino liqueur, and Amer Picon with ice, and strain into a cocktail glass. Garnish with a grapefruit twist.

GOTHAMITE

There was a time when the Gothamite was the most popular drink in Gotham City. Everyone adored its pink color and light, citrusy flavor, and bartenders couldn't keep up with demand. While its popularity has waned some since the initial craze, it is still one of the most requested cocktails at bars around town. Once you try it, you'll know why—it is irresistibly refreshing.

1½ ounces vodka

¾ ounce Cointreau

½ ounce limoncello

¾ ounce cranberry juice

1 dash orange bitters

Amarena cherry, for garnish

Shake the vodka, Cointreau, limoncello, cranberry juice, and orange bitters with ice, and strain into a cocktail glass. Garnish with an Amarena cherry.

WHITE TIE

The celebrated party cocktail, the White Tie, became an instant hit following the rumor that it was the signature drink at Thomas and Martha Wayne's wedding reception. The cocktail is notable for a few reasons: First, it is low in alcohol. Second, being light in color, it will not stain clothes or carpets. Most importantly, however, this drink is a delicious use of white port, a rarer cousin of the tawny port you might be familiar with. In this recipe, it replaces the two rums in a classic mai tai. The resulting mix is a cocktail worthy of one of Gotham City's most illustrious couples. It remains popular at fancy soirees to this day.

1½ ounces white port

½ ounce orange curaçao

½ ounce Orgeat (page 136)

1½ ounces fresh grapefruit juice

1 ounce fresh lime juice

Lime wheel, for garnish

Shake the port, curaçao, Orgeat, grapefruit juice, and lime juice with ice, and strain into a rocks glass with ice. Garnish with a lime wheel.

ONE BAD DAY

It is rumored that a particular Gotham City denizen had a very bad day when he fell into a vat of chemicals. It's even said that the green liquid turned him into The Joker. What could be in a vat that would make someone lose their mind? That is the inspiration for this cocktail, which contains both mezcal and absinthe. Sometimes called the Green Oblivion, absinthe gained its legendary reputation for inducing madness in the nineteenth century. Once banned in the United States, absinthe is now widely available. To this, Gotham City bartenders have added mind-altering mezcal—making for a saucy number that inspires, shall we say, hilarity? But beware, drink too many and the joke's on you.

1 ounce mezcal

¾ ounce Cointreau

¾ ounce elderflower liqueur

1 ounce fresh lime juice

2 dashes absinthe

Orange peel, for garnish

Shake the mezcal, Cointreau, elderflower liqueur, lime juice, and absinthe with ice, and strain into a cocktail glass. Garnish with an orange peel.

GRAY FOX

Lucius Fox has a talent for managing big projects and has a special way with finances. He is also responsible for engineering and inventing much of the high-tech equipment that has made Wayne Enterprises a billion-dollar company. This innovative cocktail is a favorite at the see-and-be-seen Royal Hotel bar in downtown Gotham City. It is an impressive specimen—bright, full of life, and with a happy garnish of a mint sprig.

2 ounces gin

½ ounce fresh pineapple juice

½ ounce fresh orange juice

½ ounce fresh lime juice

1 dash Angostura bitters

2 ounces club soda or seltzer

Fresh mint sprig, for garnish

Shake the gin, fruit juices, and Angostura bitters with ice, and strain into an ice-filled highball glass. Top with the club soda or seltzer. Garnish with a mint sprig.

MAD LOVE

This feisty cocktail is an uncommon mix of two wildly dissimilar spirits—
glamorous gin and rough tequila. The unlikely concoction works because
ginger liqueur acts as a flavor bridge, bringing two worlds colliding into
a fusion of intense flavor. If you are a fan of either the margarita or the
Dark and Stormy, this one's for you. Beware, because the Mad Love is so
deliriously delicious, it can cause quite a bit of mischief.

1 ounce gin

1 ounce tequila

¼ ounce Cointreau

¾ ounce Domaine de Canton ginger liqueur

¾ ounce fresh lime juice

Lime slice, for garnish

Shake the gin, tequila, Cointreau, Domaine de Canton, and lime juice
with ice, and strain into an ice-filled rocks glass. Cut a slice of lime into
a heart shape, and garnish.

LEVIATHAN'S KISS

An alluring drink that gets its color and flavor from a unique raspberry-rose syrup, the Leviathan's Kiss is supremely delicious . . . while it lasts. As fleeting as a summer romance, this cocktail is a huge hit on Gotham City bar menus. Rumor has it that the drink was created for Rā's al Ghūl's daughter Talia, who is as dangerous as she is beautiful. Rose water is often used in Middle Eastern cuisine, so there could be some truth to the legend. Either way, the cocktail's electrifying color and silky texture draw you into an intimate encounter you will not soon forget.

FOR THE RASPBERRY-ROSE SYRUP:

1 cup water

1 cup granulated sugar

1½ cups raspberries

4 drops rose water

FOR THE COCKTAIL:

2 ounces London dry gin

¾ ounce fresh lemon juice

¾ ounce Raspberry-Rose Syrup

1 egg white from a medium egg

Rose petals, for garnish

TO MAKE THE RASPBERRY-ROSE SYRUP: In a small saucepan, heat the water and sugar over medium heat until the sugar dissolves. Remove from the heat, add the raspberries, and mash them. Add the rose water, and let steep for 2 hours or overnight. Strain through a fine-mesh strainer, pressing the raspberry solids to extract all the juices. Store the syrup in a sealed jar in the refrigerator for up to 2 weeks.

TO MAKE THE COCKTAIL: Shake the gin, lemon juice, raspberry-rose syrup, and egg white vigorously with ice, and strain into a cocktail glass. Garnish with rose petals.

HEART OF ICE

Just looking at this bright blue cocktail will make you shiver. The Heart of Ice chills everything it touches. A twist on a daiquiri that features pineapple and coconut, this is a delightful taste of the tropics. It is a certain crowd-pleaser, especially inviting on hot days. But beware, if you drink it too fast, it will give you brain freeze!

1 ounce white rum

1 ounce blue curaçao

2 ounces fresh pineapple juice

1 ounce cream of coconut

Pineapple slice, for garnish

Shake the rum, curaçao, pineapple juice, and cream of coconut with ice, and strain into a hurricane or highball glass filled with crushed ice. Garnish with a pineapple slice. Note: To blend, combine the ingredients in a blender with 1 cup ice, and puree until smooth.

· A CITY STIRRING ·

STIRRED COCKTAILS

Drinks that do not contain citrus, eggs, or dairy are stirred in a mixing glass with ice using a barspoon. This combines and chills the ingredients without aerating them. Additionally, because these drinks are not diluted by mixers such as juices or soda, they typically have a higher ABV (alcohol by volume) than other cocktails. This class of drink is often called "spirit-forward" or "spiritous" and includes the martini, the Manhattan, the Negroni, and many more famous classics. These are cocktails that are ideal for serious, contemplative drinking sessions.

BARREL-AGING, SPIRIT-FORWARD COCKTAILS

Because the cocktails in this section contain only spirits and liqueurs, they are ideal for aging in a wood barrel, which allows a drink's ingredients to meld flavors over time. A well-made Manhattan is good, but a barrel-aged one is sublime.

It is important to not age drinks that contain citrus—without refrigeration juices will separate and spoil. Likewise, avoid bitters for aging, as they will bloom and take over the mix. Instead, add them just before you serve the aged cocktail. An easy and inexpensive way to age cocktails at home is not to use a barrel at all but a kit, which you can readily find online.

BOTANIST

Chartreuse is a green liqueur made from an ancient secret recipe. It tastes slightly vegetal while remaining refreshing. What's more, it is an important component in a number of classic cocktails such as the Last Word and the Bijou. Once you taste it, you will surely be seduced. The herbaceousness of Chartreuse is reminiscent of long, leafy fingers wrapping around your neck *and* your taste buds.

1½ ounces gin

1 ounce green Chartreuse

1 ounce blanc vermouth

1 barspoon orange curaçao

Rose petals, for garnish (optional)

Stir the gin, Chartreuse, vermouth, and curaçao with ice, and strain into a cocktail glass. Garnish with rose petals, if desired.

BITTER REVENGE

It is believed that the criminal mastermind Hush uses superior intellect to manipulate his villainous allies and exact revenge upon his enemies. Only a sophisticated drink will do for such an erudite criminal—hence this creation based on the Harvard Cooler. The traditional version combines apple brandy and lime juice, but in Gotham City it is paired with two styles of vermouth for a deliciously stiff drink.

1½ ounces Calvados

1 ounce dry vermouth

1 ounce sweet vermouth

1 dash Angostura bitters

Apple slice, for garnish

Stir the Calvados, vermouths, and Angostura bitters with ice, and strain into a cocktail glass. Garnish with an apple slice.

BIRDS OF A FEATHER

The all-female crime-fighting group Birds of Prey is formed by
Huntress, Black Canary, and Batgirl. Like a good cocktail, when the
members come together, they are more than the sum of their parts.
This is the drink for the woman who wants—and deserves—everything.
It is an elegant and potent mix that goes down like a very strong,
complex martini. Take note that the cherry-inflected Kirschwasser
makes the cocktail dry and steely rather than sweet.

1½ ounces gin

1 ounce dry vermouth

½ ounce orange curaçao

1 barspoon Kirschwasser

3 Amarena cherries

Stir the gin, vermouth, curaçao, and Kirschwasser with ice, and strain
into a cocktail glass. Garnish with the cherries on a cocktail pick.

GOTHAM CITY

While the origins of this cocktail are disputed, it is most often attributed to a party thrown in Gotham City for Mayor Thorndike while he was on the mayoral campaign trail. It was such a smash hit that the recipe was widely distributed after the party, with Gothamites clamoring to taste the signature drink of the promising contender. It is now considered a classic and a source of great civic pride. The cocktail is sure to be a favorite of those who like both whiskey sours and Manhattans.

2 ounces rye whiskey

½ ounce sweet vermouth

¼ ounce limoncello

1 dash Angostura bitters

1 lemon twist

Stir the whiskey, vermouth, limoncello, and Angostura bitters with ice, and strain into a cocktail glass. Express the lemon twist over the glass, and discard.

BLÜDHAVEN

Today we know Blüdhaven as a corrupt town that has fallen on hard times. But in the past, it was a wealthy whaling port where fancy cocktails flowed freely. After years of operating in Gotham City, Nightwing made Blüdhaven his home base, and Gotham City newspapers often report his exploits. In fact, the more famous Nightwing becomes as Blüdhaven's hero, the more popular this drink named after the city becomes.

1½ ounces gin

¾ ounce Aperol

¾ ounce dry vermouth

2 dashes Peychaud's bitters

Lemon peel, for garnish

Stir the gin, Aperol, vermouth, and Peychaud's bitters with ice, and strain into a rocks glass with a large ice cube. Garnish with a lemon peel.

ENDURING FLAME

Ace Chemical is a longtime Gotham City fixture and has been the scene of a number of events that have shaped the city into what it is today. Watch the ingredients in this curious cocktail smoke and swirl like the mysterious chemicals housed within the plant. Note that fire and alcohol do not mix, and great care should be taken in the preparation of this cocktail!

¼ ounce orange bitters

4 orange peels

2 ounces vodka

1 ounce Gran Classico bitter liqueur

½ ounce dry vermouth

Rinse a cocktail glass with the orange bitters. While squeezing an orange peel over the glass, use a match to light the oils, and place the peel in the glass. Repeat twice with 2 more orange peels. Stir the vodka, Gran Classico, and vermouth with ice in a separate glass, and strain into the prepared glass. Flame the remaining orange peel over the drink, and discard.

KING GREEN

Killer Croc was once a sideshow attraction, wrestling alligators in poorer towns across America. But then the scales started growing on his skin . . . Rumors indicate the cocktail appeared when Killer Croc's fame first spread as the new boss of the underworld. The combination of lager, rum, and simple syrup makes for a smooth start, while the lime offers a bold and refreshing finish.

1½ ounces white rum

4 ounces lager-style beer

1 ounce fresh lime juice

1 ounce Simple Syrup (page 137)

Lime wedge, for garnish

Stir the rum, beer, lime juice, and Simple Syrup with ice in a large cup. Garnish with a lime wedge.

PARK ROW

Women in furs. Men in fine suits. Jewels glittering under the marquee lights. Park Row was once one of the most glamorous streets in America, a spot where Gotham City's rich spent their weekends. This widely consumed masterpiece is a survivor of that gilded age—bold, chic, and just a little saucy. Note the drink is an exception that proves the rule—lemon juice is present in a small enough amount that the cocktail is stirred.

2 ounces gin

1 ounce sweet vermouth

1 ounce sherry (preferably fino or Manzanilla)

¼ ounce orange curaçao

¼ ounce fresh lemon juice

Lemon peel, for garnish

Stir the gin, vermouth, sherry, curaçao, and lemon juice with ice, and strain into a cocktail glass. Garnish with a lemon peel.

THE
ROMAN

Aperitivo is an Italian pre-dinner drinking ritual that includes snacks like olives and nuts accompanied by classic aperitif libations like vermouth. The Negroni is a famous example of an aperitivo cocktail—gin was added to a drink named the Americano (a blend of Campari and sweet vermouth). Italian immigrants brought their aperitivo custom to Gotham City, and it survives to this day as the Roman.

1 ounce Campari

1½ ounces sweet vermouth

½ ounce Averna

1 barspoon balsamic vinegar

1 splash club soda

2 olives

Stir the Campari, vermouth, Averna, and balsamic vinegar with ice, and strain into a rocks glass filled with ice. Top with the club soda, and garnish with the olives.

SMOKE PELLET

It's believed that Batman employs smoke pellets to confuse or stun his adversaries. This smoked cocktail captures all the mystery of Batman's sudden appearances. Smoking is a technique that adds to a drink's overall flavor, and one of the easiest materials to use is a cinnamon stick. Here, the cinnamon adds spice to a drink that is already slightly smoky from the Mexican chile liqueur, Ancho Reyes, which is readily available in liquor stores and online.

1 cinnamon stick

2 ounces blended scotch

¾ ounce Averna

½ ounce Ancho Reyes

1 dash Peychaud's bitters

1 lemon twist

Chill a rocks glass, then smoke-rinse it by lighting the cinnamon stick and covering with the upside-down glass. Note: Use a kitchen torch to light the cinnamon, as lighter fluid will impart a chemical flavor to the smoke. In a mixing glass, stir the scotch, Averna, Ancho Reyes, and Peychaud's bitters with ice, and strain into the prepared rocks glass. Express the lemon twist over the drink, and discard.

SAKURA

Sakura is the name for Japanese cherry tree blossoms. The flowers are often made into syrups and liqueurs that are prized in cocktails. Here, the subtle cherry flavor is a perfect foil for gin's herbal notes. The sake in this recipe can be replaced with dry white wine for a similarly rounded taste and feel, although the flavor and texture will differ. Cherry blossom syrup is widely available in grocery stores and online. When combined, these ingredients form a drink as cool and smooth as the blade of the Soultaker.

1 ounce gin

1 ounce sake

¾ ounce dry vermouth

1 barspoon fresh lemon juice

1 barspoon cherry blossom syrup

1 barspoon Kirschwasser

Amarena cherry, for garnish

Stir the gin, sake, vermouth, lemon juice, cherry blossom syrup, and Kirschwasser with ice, and strain into a cocktail glass. Garnish with a cherry.

FIRST FOE

Steven Crane, Alfred Stryker, and Paul Rogers were Batman's first criminal adversaries. An enterprising Gotham City bartender was quick to create a martini when news of the foes' encounter spread through the city, an homage to an event that would change Gotham City forever. Appreciative and nostalgic citizens frequently order the cocktail to this day.

2 ounces London dry gin

¾ ounce dry vermouth

¼ ounce Cointreau

1 dash Angostura bitters

Orange twist, for garnish

Stir the gin, vermouth, Cointreau, and Angostura bitters with ice, and strain into a cocktail glass. Garnish with an orange twist.

TALONS OUT

The Court of Owls is a secretive criminal society that is believed to have existed in Gotham City since the town was a fledgling colony. The group is infamous for indoctrinating new members and forcing them to become assassins known as the Talons. This cocktail is often associated with the group and combines two early colonial ingredients—rum and curaçao. Curaçao was wildly popular in Gotham City's early years, a gift from Dutch settlers. Because a group of owls is called a "parliament," you will sometimes see this alternative name for the drink on menus.

2 ounces rum (such as Mount Gay or Pusser's)

1 ounce orange curaçao

½ ounce fresh lime juice

1 ounce club soda

Freshly grated nutmeg, for garnish

Stir the rum, curaçao, and lime juice with ice, and strain into an ice-filled rocks glass. Add the club soda, and garnish with nutmeg.

THE
TUXEDO

Why do penguins wear tuxedos? The flightless birds look as if they are all dressed up and ready for a night out on the town. The tuxedo—the formal garment—gets its name from the Tuxedo Club in the Hudson Valley where the clothing style was popularized in America. The club also bequeathed us a famous cocktail, the eponymously named Tuxedo. This version is a Gotham City favorite, rumored to have been invented at the rakish Iceberg Lounge.

¾ ounce vodka

¾ ounce London dry gin

¾ ounce dry vermouth (preferably Noilly Prat)

1 barspoon maraschino liqueur

Grapefruit peel, for garnish

Stir the vodka, gin, vermouth, and maraschino liqueur with ice, and strain into a chilled cocktail glass. Garnish with a grapefruit peel.

UTILITY BELT

FILLS A 6-OUNCE FLASK

It is believed that Batman uses many gadgets to aid him in his war on crime.
In order to carry these items on his person, it's said that he wears a "Utility
Belt" of sorts. This Utility Belt is one of Batman's key pieces of equipment
for fighting crime, just as this flask cocktail is an essential offering of
drinkeries throughout Gotham City. It is redolent of clove, pepper, nutmeg,
and cinnamon, making the drink a great fireside sipper.

3½ ounces Laird's applejack

1½ ounces St. Elizabeth Allspice Dram

¾ ounce dry vermouth

Stir the applejack, Allspice Dram, and vermouth with ice,
and strain into a hip flask.

· ONE PUNCH ·

PUNCHES, PARTY BOWLS, AND TEAS

It is thought the word *punch* comes from the Hindu word *paunch*, which means *five things*—liquor, lemon, sugar, water, and tea. The invention was brought from India to England by sailors in the British East India Company. From there it traveled on to the American colonies and Gotham City. After the American Revolutionary War, punch fell out of favor and was reserved for holidays and special occasions. Punch makes entertaining a snap; mixing up a batch of drinks in advance frees you to spend time with your guests instead of bartending.

FORTUNE TELLER

MAKES 4 TO 6 SERVINGS

Immortal mystic Madame Xanadu channels her powers of premonition through tarot cards. The aroma of this alluring tea is reminiscent of the scent that lingers in the air inside the cloistered walls of her shop. The warming brew features orange blossom water and rose water, two ingredients that provide robust flavor. They are available at Middle Eastern grocery stores. Serve this drink from a teapot to complete the experience.

2 mint tea bags

2 cups boiling water

1 cup gin

¼ cup Simple Syrup (page 137)

4 dashes orange blossom water

2 dashes rose water

Fresh mint leaves, for garnish

Lemon wheels, for garnish

Steep the tea bags with 2 cups boiling water according to the package instructions. Add the gin, Simple Syrup, orange blossom water, and rose water, and stir. To serve, tear a few mint leaves into each individual teacup, and pour the tea mixture over them. Garnish each cup with a lemon wheel.

ICEBERG PUNCH

MAKES 6 SERVINGS

The Iceberg Lounge's punch is a version of a white sangria, as the bar's mixologist wanted a colorless version of the Spanish classic so it would not stain his club's carpet. Additionally, he hated the idea of red wine spilling on guests' dress shirts. White sangria is a light variation, particularly refreshing on a hot day. Plus, all the fruit makes for an attractive presentation.

1 lime, sliced

1 lemon, sliced

¼ cup granulated sugar

¼ cup dry vermouth

One 750-ml bottle white
  wine

½ green apple, diced

1 peach, sliced

½ cup strawberries,
  sliced

Fresh mint sprigs,
  for garnish

Gently muddle the lime, lemon, and sugar in a large pitcher. Add the vermouth, white wine, apple, peach, and strawberries, and stir. Add ice, and stir. Garnish individual punch glasses with mint sprigs.

SERIOUS HOUSE PUNCH

MAKES 6 TO 8 SERVINGS

"Serious House" is the nickname for Arkham Asylum, the institution for the criminally insane that houses some of Gotham City's worst super-villains. Legend has it this punch recipe was concocted by the asylum's guards as a way to toast the arrival of new inmates—after all, every new "guest" was additional job security.

2 cups aged rum

¾ cup fresh lime juice

¾ cup fresh pineapple juice

½ cup Simple Syrup (page 137)

6 dashes pimento bitters (Angostura is a fine substitute)

1 cup seltzer

Lime slices, for garnish

Stir together the rum, lime juice, pineapple juice, Simple Syrup, and pimento bitters in a large pitcher. Refrigerate until chilled. Transfer to a punch bowl, and add the seltzer. Garnish individual glasses with a lime slice.

REMARKABLE RUSE

MAKES 4 TO 6 SERVINGS

Guessing the key ingredient in this large-format party cocktail is part of the fun. The secret is simple but can be hard to guess: a few whole cloves soaked in bourbon. The resulting flavor makes for a novel, spice-forward drink and provides a certain je ne sais quoi that will stump most sippers. When serving, consider giving an award to the guest who solves the flavor riddle first.

FOR THE CLOVE-INFUSED BOURBON:

4 cloves

1 cup bourbon

FOR THE COCKTAIL:

3 black tea bags

1 cup boiling water

½ cup Simple Syrup (page 137)

½ cup fresh lemon juice

1 cup Clove-Infused Bourbon

6 dashes Angostura bitters

Lemon slices, for garnish

Fresh mint leaves, for garnish

TO MAKE THE CLOVE-INFUSED BOURBON: In a medium sealable jar, combine the cloves and bourbon. Let stand for 4 days and remove cloves before using.

TO MAKE THE COCKTAIL: Combine the tea bags and 1 cup boiling water, steep for 5 minutes, and let cool. In a punch bowl, combine the tea, Simple Syrup, and lemon juice, and stir. Add the clove-infused bourbon, bitters, and 1 cup of ice cubes. Stir until the ice is melted and the punch is cold. Garnish with lemon slices and mint leaves, and serve in cups.

SLEIGH RIDE

MAKES 6 TO 8 SERVINGS

The holidays are a great time of year; there are so many smiles and so many opportunities for mischief. What better way to have a few laughs with friends than to gather around a punch bowl? This delightful punch is similar to eggnog but with a big difference—there is no cream or egg. This means it has all the flavor and texture but none of the calories or lingering heaviness. Tired of feeling full after one round of eggnog? Never again! Now that will bring out your sensahumah!

1 cup dark rum

1 cup brandy

½ cup granulated sugar

1 tablespoon vanilla extract

½ gallon whole milk

Freshly grated nutmeg, for garnish

Freshly grated cinnamon, for garnish

Stir together the rum, brandy, sugar, and vanilla extract in a pitcher until the sugar dissolves. Add milk, stir, and place in the freezer until cold and slushy, 4 to 6 hours. Stir to break up the ice, pour into glasses, and garnish each glass with nutmeg and cinnamon.

DIGESTIFS AND HANGOVER CURES

This chapter contains both so-called "hair of the dog" cocktails as well as popular Gotham City after-dinner sippers. You will find versions of the mimosa, Bloody Mary, Corpse Reviver, and espresso martini, as well as a spicy take on the mudslide. While these drinks are typically consumed at brunch or late in the evening, they are great any time of day.

ACE FIZZ

If you like mimosas, you will love this version of a Buck's Fizz. The Buck's Fizz is similar to a mimosa except it contains double the amount of champagne. The Ace Fizz goes one step further, with a touch of lemon juice for brightness and a dash of Galliano for vanilla notes. This will be your new brunch favorite, as it is at all of Gotham City's best restaurants.

3 ounces champagne

1½ ounces fresh orange juice

½ ounce fresh lemon juice

1 dash Galliano

Lemon twist, for garnish

Combine the champagne, orange juice, lemon juice, and Galliano in a champagne flute. Garnish with a lemon twist.

FINNIGAN'S

As day turns to night in Gotham City, the gents at the bar Finnigan's—who tend to be police officers—crave a jolt. They get it from this, the establishment's signature drink, the famed Finnigan's coffee cocktail. It is the best espresso martini in Gotham City, and if you say otherwise within earshot of the bar, you might find yourself in a bit of trouble.

1 ounce vodka

1 ounce cold espresso

1 ounce Kahlúa

½ ounce crème de cacao

1 fresh mint sprig

Shake the vodka, espresso, Kahlúa, crème de cacao, and mint sprig with ice, and strain into a cocktail glass.

EARLY BIRD

This bracing cocktail is one of the leading sellers at the Iceberg Lounge's weekend brunch cabaret shows. It has become well-known all over Gotham City and is even served at fancier spots. Think of it as a cousin to the salty dog but with gin. The Early Bird is delicious and refreshing but also a mighty effective hangover cure, which likely explains its popularity as a morning drink.

2 ounces London dry gin

3 ounces fresh grapefruit juice

½ ounce fresh lime juice

¼ ounce maraschino liqueur

2 ounces club soda

Grapefruit twist, for garnish

Shake the gin, grapefruit juice, lime juice, and maraschino liqueur with ice, and strain into an ice-filled highball glass. Top with the club soda, and garnish with a grapefruit twist.

CRIMSON MIST

Gotham City is tough. On Sunday mornings, as diners shove off the haze of sleep and head out to brunch, police are often still piecing together clues of the previous night's criminal activities. Gothamites sure have a dark sense of humor because this cocktail is one of the most popular weekend libations.

2 ounces tequila

4 ounces fresh tomato juice

½ ounce fresh lemon juice

3 drops Tabasco

1 dash Worcestershire sauce

1 dash Angostura bitters

Freshly ground black pepper, for garnish

Lemon wedge, for garnish

Shake the tequila, tomato juice, lemon juice, Tabasco, Worcestershire sauce, and bitters with ice, and strain into an ice-filled highball glass. Garnish with a dash of black pepper and a lemon wedge.

OVERACTING

When rumors of actor Basil Karlo's descent into madness began circulating throughout Gotham City, bartenders who knew him from his improv troupe days created this drink. Now the city's theatergoers order the cocktail and swap theories about the once-great entertainer. The combination of spice and coffee makes this a deliciously rich sipper.

2 ounces bourbon

1 ounce Kahlúa

½ ounce Fireball liqueur

1 dash heavy cream

Combine the bourbon, Kahlúa, and Fireball in an ice-filled rocks glass.
Add the cream, and stir.

LAZARUS

According to whispered rumors passed among bartenders and waitstaff throughout Gotham City, the Lazarus Pits are mysterious chemical pools that Rā's al Ghūl is said to have used to regenerate himself over the centuries. For mortals looking for revival, this cocktail is a safer bet. Tart citrus balances the liqueur with an invigorating brightness. This drink is guaranteed to bring you back to life after a big night.

¼ ounce absinthe

1 ounce London dry gin

1 ounce Cointreau

1 ounce dry vermouth

1 ounce fresh lemon juice

Rinse a cocktail glass with the absinthe. Shake the gin, Cointreau, vermouth, and lemon juice with ice, and strain into the prepared glass.

ESSENTIAL SNACKS

Gotham City is a big food town. It boasts every type of establishment, from fancy restaurants that receive national acclaim to diners serving humble classics. In fact, if Gothamites have anything in common, it is that they love to eat. In this chapter, you will find some of Gotham City's most important recipes, such as the popcorn from the city's famous movie theater, popular fundraiser snacks, and a few Wayne family favorites—because what is served at Wayne Manor inevitably makes its way into newspaper food columns. The bites collected here are versatile, good for hosting both big parties and intimate nights at home. And, of course, they pair well with cocktails.

MONARCH THEATER POPCORN

MAKES 2 TO 4 SERVINGS

The famed Monarch Theater may have closed, but as a consolation, Gotham City's film buffs can still prepare its famous popcorn. This recipe shows it's easy to make movie night extra special by employing a few common pantry items. The addition of citrus zest makes for a bright, flavorful, crave-worthy snack. Note the best oils to use are either coconut or grapeseed, but vegetable oil or olive oil will also work.

½ cup unpopped popcorn

2 tablespoons coconut oil

½ teaspoon Old Bay seasoning

½ teaspoon curry powder

Kosher salt and freshly ground black pepper

Lime zest, for garnish

In a half-cup measuring cup, combine the popcorn and oil to coat the kernels. Place a medium saucepan over medium heat, add the popcorn, and cover with the lid. Shaking occasionally, cook the popcorn until the pops slow to 1 to 2 seconds in between.

Pour popcorn into a paper bag, and add the Old Bay seasoning, curry powder, and salt and black pepper to taste. Toss, garnish with lime zest, and serve in a bowl.

GALA CROSTINI

MAKES 16 CROSTINI (6 TO 8 SERVINGS)

These Italian-inspired roast beef snacks appear so frequently at Gotham City galas that they are often referred to as "fundraisers." It is easy to see why they are so popular; the combination of beef, peperoncini and red pepper relish, and goat cheese makes for an addictive, flavorful snack that can also work as a light meal.

¼ cup roasted red peppers, minced

3 peperoncini, minced

1½ teaspoons dried thyme

1½ teaspoons red wine vinegar

Sixteen ¼-inch-thick diagonal baguette slices, toasted

5 ounces fresh goat cheese, at room temperature

1 ounce baby arugula

16 slices rare roast beef

In a small bowl, mix the red peppers, peperoncini, thyme, and vinegar. Spread this relish thinly on the toasted baguette slices, reserving 2 tablespoons for garnish. Spread the goat cheese over the relish, reserving 2 tablespoons cheese for garnish. Top the cheese with the arugula. Fold the roast beef slices, and place on top of the arugula. Top the beef with a bit of the remaining goat cheese, and garnish with the remaining relish. Arrange the crostini on a platter, and serve.

OPERA INTERMISSION SNACK MIX

MAKES 6 TO 8 SERVINGS

Bruce Wayne's father, Thomas, loved going to the Gotham City Opera. He is noted to have loved the sets, the costumes, the drama, and, of course, the arias. When reminiscing about the opera, Bruce has said that he often accompanied his father— but while he eventually started to enjoy the pageantry, he mostly looked forward to the intermission snacks. He is not alone; for many operagoers, this smoky and sweet blend is a highlight of the long performances.

One 12-ounce box rice squares cereal (about 10 cups)

1½ cups Asian rice cracker mix

1½ cups mini pretzels

1 cup smoked almonds

¼ cup soy sauce

½ cup maple syrup

2 sticks (1 cup) unsalted butter

½ teaspoon garlic powder

Freshly ground black pepper

Kosher salt

Preheat the oven to 300°F. Line 2 large rimmed baking sheets with parchment paper.

In a large bowl, combine the cereal, cracker mix, pretzels, and almonds. In a medium saucepan over medium heat, combine the soy sauce, maple syrup, butter, garlic powder, and black pepper, and bring to a simmer. Pour the mixture over the snack mix, and toss to coat evenly. Spread evenly on the prepared baking sheets, and bake for 30 minutes, stirring 2 or 3 times, or until nearly dry and toasted.

Let cool on the baking sheets completely before serving, stirring occasionally. Finish with additional salt and black pepper to taste.

ROYAL HOTEL BAR NUTS

MAKES 6 TO 8 SERVINGS

Many an appetite has been ruined by sitting at Gotham City's famed Royal Hotel bar—the nuts are that addictive. Incredibly, the hotel published the recipe in the *Gotham City Gazette* a few years ago, and it is reprinted here. The secret to the addictive snack is Angostura bitters, a common cocktail ingredient. The nuts are a cinch to make and the perfect accompaniment to mixed drinks. What's more, this is a great fix for a hunger emergency—prepare a few batches and keep them on hand whenever you need a delicious crowd-pleaser! Store in an airtight container at room temperature for up to one week, in the refrigerator for up to three weeks, and in the freezer for up to two months.

1 egg white

1 tablespoon Angostura bitters

½ teaspoon vanilla extract

1 cup granulated sugar

1 teaspoon kosher salt

½ teaspoon ground cinnamon

1 pound raw pecan halves

Preheat the oven to 300°F. Grease a baking sheet with butter or line with parchment paper.

In a medium bowl, whip the egg white until frothy. Mix in the bitters and vanilla extract. In a separate medium bowl, combine the sugar, salt, and cinnamon. Add the pecans to the egg white mixture, stirring to coat the nuts evenly. Next, pour the nuts into the sugar mixture, and toss until coated. Spread the nuts evenly on the prepared baking sheet, and bake for 1 hour, stirring every 15 minutes.

Remove the nuts, and move to a cooling rack until ready to serve.

PROPER CUCUMBER SANDWICHES

MAKES 12 SANDWICHES (4 TO 6 SERVINGS)

These classic English sandwiches are traditionally served with tea. They were a favorite of businessman Thomas Wayne, and the recipe comes from his butler Alfred Pennyworth. It is amazing how, when the perfectly assembled sandwiches are arranged into neat stacks, the entire world seems to be in order, if only for a moment.

2½ tablespoons salted butter, at room temperature

6 slices white bread

2½ tablespoons cream cheese, at room temperature

1 English cucumber, peeled and sliced into thin rounds

2 tablespoons finely chopped fresh dill

¼ teaspoon kosher salt

¼ teaspoon freshly ground black pepper

Spread the butter on one side of 3 slices of bread, and spread the cream cheese on one side of the remaining 3 slices. Layer the cucumber slices onto the buttered breads, and sprinkle with the dill, salt, and black pepper. Place the bread slices with cream cheese on top of the cucumber with the cream cheese side down. Cut off the crusts from the sandwiches, and cut each sandwich diagonally into 4 quarters.

MARTHA WAYNE'S CRAB RÉMOULADE

MAKES 6 TO 8 SERVINGS

Crab is plentiful in the waters off Gotham City, and this dip is an ever-popular party appetizer. Philanthropist Martha Wayne's recipe is by far the town's most famous version. Rémoulade is a classic French sauce that gained popularity in the United States in the eighteenth century. The sauce's vinegary, herbaceous flavor makes it a perfect foil for seafood. It is a cinch to prepare and will wow guests.

½ cup mayonnaise

2 tablespoons olive oil

2 teaspoons white wine vinegar

1 teaspoon Dijon mustard

1 teaspoon capers, drained

½ teaspoon finely chopped
   fresh flat-leaf parsley

½ teaspoon granulated sugar

½ teaspoon kosher salt

⅛ teaspoon freshly ground
   black pepper

3 green onions, finely chopped

¼ cup grilled corn kernels
   (optional)

1 pound jumbo lump crabmeat

Crackers, for serving

In a medium bowl, mix together the mayonnaise, olive oil, vinegar, mustard, capers, parsley, sugar, salt, black pepper, green onions, and corn, if using. Add the crab and gently fold into the mixture. Serve with crackers.

GOTHAM CITY WINGS

MAKES 5 SERVINGS

These jet-black "bat" wings are wildly popular in Gotham City, especially around Halloween. Although spooky and even a little alarming, they are so delicious, they will win over kids and adults alike. Be sure to pop the joints on the wings by bending them backward in order to stretch them out to their full bat-like potential—and be mindful of the food coloring; it stains clothes and counters. This is a dramatic, unforgettable presentation that works as an appetizer or a full meal.

½ cup ketchup

¼ cup apple cider vinegar

2 tablespoons soy sauce

2 tablespoons honey

1 teaspoon garlic powder

1 tablespoon Old Bay seasoning

1 tablespoon hot pepper sauce

¼ teaspoon black food coloring gel

½ teaspoon kosher salt

¼ teaspoon freshly ground black pepper

3 pounds whole chicken wings with tips

In a large freezer bag, combine the ketchup, vinegar, soy sauce, honey, garlic powder, Old Bay seasoning, hot pepper sauce, food coloring, salt, and black pepper. Add the chicken, and coat with the marinade. Seal the bag, and marinate the wings in the refrigerator for 1 to 2 hours.

Preheat the oven to 375°F. Line a baking sheet with aluminum foil. Place the wings on the prepared baking sheet, with the underside of the wings facing up, and reserve the marinade in the refrigerator. Roast for 20 minutes, then flip the wings, brush with the remaining marinade, and roast for 20 minutes more, or until cooked through. Finish cooking under the broiler for 5 minutes more, to crisp the skin.

ESPRESSO NOCTURNS

MAKES 8 TO 12 SERVINGS

This recipe is one of Gotham City's best-kept catering secrets. If you are looking for an easy, rich, and crowd-pleasing dessert, this is it. Unlike most pot de crème recipes, these dark chocolate espresso pots do not require a fussy double boiler, nor do they contain eggs. This means they are a cinch to make and are a cocktail-party hit. Serve them in shot glasses for an extra-simple presentation.

1 cup heavy cream

2 ounces espresso (a double shot)

4 dashes Angostura bitters

1½ tablespoons granulated sugar

¼ teaspoon kosher salt

4 ounces dark chocolate, finely chopped

Orange zest, for garnish

In a medium saucepan over medium-high heat, heat the cream, espresso, Angostura bitters, sugar, and salt to near boiling, stirring to combine. Remove from the heat, add the chocolate, and whisk thoroughly until the mixture is smooth. Transfer the mixture to a liquid measuring cup for easy pouring, and pour into espresso cups or shot glasses.

Refrigerate, covered, for 2 hours or overnight. Garnish with orange zest before serving.

MANOR MULLIGATAWNY

MAKES 6 SERVINGS

If you have ever been lucky enough to be invited to Wayne Manor, you know this dish. Mulligatawny is a well-known soup that blends English and Indian cuisines. It became popular with the British stationed in India during colonial times, and from there it spread around the world. The delicious one-pot meal is a bit spicy with just a hint of sweetness. It is also warming, nutritious, and comforting. As a bonus, it tastes better the next day, making it a perfect dish to assemble ahead.

2 tablespoons coconut oil or olive oil

1 medium yellow onion, finely chopped

1 cup finely diced carrots

2 celery stalks, chopped

2 garlic cloves, minced

1 white turnip, peeled and chopped

3 tablespoons curry powder

1 teaspoon ground cumin

1 teaspoon ground turmeric

1 teaspoon kosher salt

1 teaspoon freshly ground black pepper

Two 15-ounce cans chickpeas, drained
and rinsed

6 cups chicken stock, divided

½ cup coconut milk

2 cups shredded cooked chicken (optional)

¼ cup finely chopped fresh cilantro

In a large saucepan over medium-high heat, heat the oil. Add the onion, carrots, celery, garlic, and turnip, and cook, stirring occasionally, for about 10 minutes, or until the vegetables begin to soften.

Add the curry powder, cumin, turmeric, salt, pepper, 1 can of the chickpeas, and 4 cups of the chicken stock. Bring to a boil, then lower the heat to a simmer.

Meanwhile, in a blender, combine the remaining can of chickpeas and 2 cups stock, and puree until smooth. Add the blended chickpea mixture and coconut milk to the soup, and stir to combine.

Add chicken, if desired. Stir well, and continue to simmer until the flavors meld for 10 minutes. Serve in bowls, and garnish with cilantro.

BARBARA GORDON'S LEMON CHICKEN

MAKES 4 TO 6 SERVINGS

Barbara Gordon's lemon chicken recipe is famous at the Gotham City Police Department. It is a running joke that if James Gordon cannot be found, it's best to assume Barbara has made her chicken. It is that good. This recipe is based on a dish that was once called chicken française, which was prepared by dredging chicken cutlets in egg and flour, then pan-frying them. This simplified version uses more flavorful thighs instead of breast meat and is also carb- and gluten-free.

2 tablespoons olive oil

2 teaspoons lemon zest

2 tablespoons fresh lemon juice

½ cup dry white wine

2 garlic cloves, minced

1 teaspoon kosher salt

1 teaspoon freshly ground black pepper

4 pounds skin-on chicken thighs

2 tablespoons unsalted butter

1 pinch paprika

4 to 6 lemon slices

In a large glass dish or large freezer bag, combine the olive oil, lemon zest, lemon juice, white wine, garlic, salt, and black pepper. Poke holes in the chicken with a fork, add to the marinade, and refrigerate for 1 to 2 hours.

Preheat the oven to 400°F. Line a rimmed baking sheet with aluminum foil.

Place the chicken thighs, skin side up, on the prepared baking sheet, reserving the marinade in the refrigerator.

Roast for 20 minutes, then baste with some of the remaining marinade. Roast for 20 minutes more, or until the chicken is cooked to an internal temperature of 165°F and the skin is starting to brown. If you desire crispier skin, switch the oven to broil for an extra 5 minutes. Remove the thighs from the oven, tent with foil, and let rest for 10 minutes.

In a small saucepan over medium-high heat, bring the remaining marinade to a boil, and lower heat to a simmer for 10 minutes (it won't look like much, that is okay!). Add the butter to the sauce, and cook until melted.

To serve, place the thighs on a plate alone or with rice, pasta, or mashed potatoes, and pour the sauce over the dish. Garnish with the paprika and lemon slices.

BATARANG BROWNIES

MAKES ABOUT 16 BATARANGS (6 TO 8 SERVINGS)

These flavorful bites were introduced at a Wayne Manor holiday party and have since become a Gotham City staple. No one knows for sure who thought to make brownies in the shape of Batarangs, but they were a huge hit with guests. In fact, newspapers reported that the mayor ate five brownies. Note that bat-shaped cookie cutters are available at kitchen stores and online.

2 sticks (1 cup) unsalted butter

4 ounces unsweetened chocolate, chopped

2 cups granulated sugar

¼ cup molasses

4 eggs, beaten

1 teaspoon vanilla extract

½ cup all-purpose flour

3 teaspoons cocoa powder

½ teaspoon baking powder

2 tablespoons ground ginger

¼ teaspoon kosher salt

Preheat the oven to 350°F. Butter a rimmed 18-by-13-inch baking sheet.

In a medium saucepan over medium-low heat, melt the butter and chocolate together, stirring constantly until blended. Remove from the heat, and stir in the sugar and molasses. Add the eggs and vanilla, and stir until smooth. Add the flour, cocoa powder, baking powder, ginger, and salt, and stir to combine.

Pour the batter into the prepared baking sheet. Bake for 30 to 35 minutes, or until a toothpick inserted into the center comes out clean. Let cool, then cut the brownies with a bat-shaped cookie cutter, or cut into squares with a knife.

COCKTAIL PANTRY

AMARENA CHERRIES

Amarena cherries have become the staple for bartenders over the past twenty years. There are a few brands making decent maraschino cherries—avoid the sugary, dyed versions unless you intentionally want to be retro and campy.

BATCHING

Any individually sized drink recipe can be batched by converting ounces to cups.

BITTERS

Angostura bitters, Peychaud's bitters, and orange bitters—all three are necessary for a number of classic cocktails, and it is worth having them on hand.

CARBONATED WATER

Club soda, seltzer water, and mineral water can all be used in cocktails, but they are not identical. Club soda includes additives—often sodium and potassium for additional flavor. Seltzer is simply water that has been carbonated, and mineral water is bottled from naturally occurring springs. Typically, bartenders use club soda for cocktails.

EGGS

Do not fear raw eggs; they make for incredible texture in cocktails. To prevent any shells from getting into your drink, never crack eggs on the edge of the shaker; instead, crack gently on a hard, clean surface. If you have a compromised immune system, consider powdered egg whites: 2 teaspoons powder to 1 ounce water will approximate a single white. As an alternative to eggs, chickpea cooking water—called aquafaba—will yield a similar froth. Three tablespoons is equivalent to approximately one egg white.

ICE

Ice is an often overlooked but crucial ingredient in cocktails. Because it takes on other flavors from the freezer, be sure to make it fresh. It is also worth using filtered water. Invest in a few silicone ice cube trays if you want nice squares. For making drinks with crushed ice, pick up a Lewis bag and mallet.

MUDDLING

Muddle to express the oils in citrus and herbs. Apply pressure for citrus, but use gentle force for herbs. There is nothing worse than getting tiny mint pieces stuck in your teeth because leaves have been pulverized. Overmuddling can also impart an unpleasant bitterness to your drink.

NUTMEG

Nutmeg is a quintessential cocktail ingredient and appears as a garnish grated over a number of classic drinks. It is good to keep a few whole nutmegs on hand and grate them using a Microplane.

OLIVES

Spanish Manzanilla olives are the classic cocktail garnish in the United States. However, juicy Castelvetrano olives give them a run for their money, and it is worth procuring a jar for your cocktail pantry. They are also a perfect accompaniment to antipasti or added to a salad with feta cheese. You may never go back.

ORANGE BLOSSOM WATER

Orange blossom water is necessary for orgeat (see below) and is crucial in the Ramos gin fizz, the pisco sour, and other classics. It can also serve as a flavorful addition to hot tea cocktails such as the Fortune Teller (page 99).

ORGEAT

Orgeat is a cloudy almond syrup that often includes orange blossom water or rose water. Traditionally, it was a summer drink consumed on its own or mixed with liqueurs. Orgeat is available in liquor stores and online, but it is better and cheaper to make your own. There are a number of complex recipes that involve squeezing soaked almonds to get milk; avoid the hassle with the following recipe.

Makes about 1 cup

½ cup sugar (demerara or cane sugar is best, but white granulated sugar is fine)

Peel of half a grapefruit · 1 scant cup almond milk

8 drops almond extract · 4 drops orange blossom water

In a medium sealable jar, combine the sugar and grapefruit peel, and macerate for 1 to 2 hours, until the citrus oils have begun to soak into the sugar. Add the almond milk, and remove the peel. Add the almond extract and orange blossom water, seal the jar, and shake the mixture until the sugar dissolves. Orgeat will keep sealed in the refrigerator for about 1 week.

RINSING A GLASS

You can rinse a glass by pouring a small amount of liqueur into it and then rolling the glass around so it is coated. Alternatively, bartenders will put ice in the glass, and then pour the rinsing liqueur over it. They will then construct the drink in a separate glass, return to the first glass, swirl the flavored ice, and discard both, and pour the drink into the rinsed glass—thereby chilling the glass and rinsing it at the same time.

ROSE WATER

Rose water is available at many Middle Eastern markets. It is a staple for a complete cocktail pantry and appears in a few modern classics.

SHAKING

As a general rule, cocktails that contain citrus, eggs, or dairy are shaken. Sometimes, eggs are shaken alone in the shaker first, and this is called a dry shake.

SIMPLE SYRUP

Simple syrup can be made with a variety of sugars. Granulated white sugar will impart the least flavor and is appropriate for most drinks. The rich taste of demerara sugar is perfect for many rum and whiskey drinks. Note that some cocktails will call for "rich" simple syrup, which means a ratio of 2 to 1 sugar to water instead of 1 to 1. The method for making simple syrup for most cocktails, and the drinks in this book, is below.

1 cup water • 1 cup granulated sugar

In a small saucepan over high heat, heat the water until near boiling. Remove the pan from the heat, add the sugar, and stir until dissolved. Let the syrup cool, and transfer to a medium sealable jar. Refrigerate for up to 1 month.

STIRRING

Stir cocktails that are spirits only, such as martinis. Stirring blends and cools a cocktail without aerating it.

SUGARS

Most classic cocktails—and simple syrups (see above)—are best made with granulated white sugar. Natural, unbleached, or raw sugars are good for drinks that can handle extra flavor. A good compromise between the two is organic unbleached sugar, which won't impart too many molasses and vanilla notes. A well-stocked cocktail pantry should also have sugar cubes on hand for old-fashioneds and Sazeracs (in this book, they are used in the Gotham City Royal, Old Gotham, Narrows Original, and Suit Up drinks). A popular sugar cube brand with bartenders is La Perruche. Other common sweeteners that are great in cocktails are maple syrup and cane sugar syrup.

TEMPERATURE

Temperature is a key component of great cocktails, and having a couple of glasses in the freezer at the ready or microwaving a mug for a few seconds will do wonders.

Acknowledgments

A heartfelt thank-you is owed to my editor, Maya Alpert and associate editor, Anna Wostenberg for their astute suggestions, additions, and fixes during this project. Plus, a big thank-you to my agent, Clare Pelino for her continued guidance and support.

Ed Burke assisted with research, and I thank him for his time, passion, and insight.

A big thank-you to Kevin Lundell of Broad Street Beverage Co. who assisted with recipe testing and gave excellent advice on the cocktails in this book.

A giant thanks is owed to my partner Janine Hawley, who bakes more Batman brownies than one household can consume—almost.

A debt of gratitude is also owed to those who have breathed the ink and interpreted the Batman material. Of particular inspiration to me in writing this book: Bill Finger, Frank Miller, Jeph Loeb, Dennis O'Neil, Jim Lee, Jim Starlin, Grant Morrison, Scott Snyder, Alan Moore, and Neil Gaiman.

Also, a note of sincere thanks to illustrator Bill Lutz; it is unlikely I would have come down this road without our collaboration.

Finally, a giant thank-you is due to my parents, Mahlon and Sonja Darlington, who gave me a Batman cape those many years ago.

Also by André Darlington

Booze Cruise: A Tour of the World's Essential Mixed Drinks

Booze and Vinyl

The New Cocktail Hour

TCM's Movie Night Menus

The Prettiest Star

China Bus

NOTES

NOTES

INSIGHT
EDITIONS

PO Box 3088
San Rafael, CA 94912
www.insighteditions.com

 Find us on Facebook: www.facebook.com/InsightEditions

 Follow us on Twitter: @insighteditions

Library of Congress Cataloging-in-Publication Data available.

ISBN: 978-1-64722-181-2

Publisher: Raoul Goff
VP of Licensing and Partnerships: Vanessa Lopez
VP of Creative: Chrissy Kwasnik
VP of Manufacturing: Alix Nicholaeff
Designer: Monique Narboneta
Editor: Maya Alpert
Associate Editor: Anna Wostenberg
Managing Editor: Lauren LePera
Production Editor: Jennifer Bentham
Production Manager: Eden Orlesky
Senior Production Manager, Subsidiary Rights: Lina s Palma

Photographer: Ted Thomas
Food and Prop Stylist: Elena P. Craig
Prop Stylist Assistant: August Craig

ROOTS of PEACE   REPLANTED PAPER

Insight Editions, in association with Roots of Peace, will plant two trees for each tree
used in the manufacturing of this book. Roots of Peace is an internationally renowned
humanitarian organization dedicated to eradicating land mines worldwide and converting
war-torn lands into productive farms and wildlife habitats. Roots of Peace will plant two
million fruit and nut trees in Afghanistan and provide farmers there with the skills and
support necessary for sustainable land use.

Manufactured in Turkey by Insight Editions
10 9 8 7 6 5 4 3